BERKELEY'S *A TREATISE CONCERNING THE PRINCIPLES OF HUMAN KNOWLEDGE*

George Berkeley's *A Treatise Concerning the Principles of Human Knowledge* is a crucial text in the history of empiricism and in the history of philosophy more generally. Its central and seemingly astonishing claim is that the physical world cannot exist independently of the perceiving mind. The meaning of this claim, the powerful arguments in its favour, and the system in which it is embedded are explained in a highly lucid and readable manner and placed in their historical context. Berkeley's philosophy is, in part, a response to the deep tensions and problems in the new philosophy of the early modern period, and the reader is offered an account of this intellectual milieu. The book then follows the order and substance of the *Principles* while drawing on materials from Berkeley's other writings. This volume is the ideal introduction to Berkeley's *Principles* and will be of great interest to historians of philosophy in general.

P. J. E. KAIL is University Lecturer in the History of Modern Philosophy, University of Oxford, and Fellow and Tutor in Philosophy at St Peter's College, Oxford. He is co-editor with Marina Frasca-Spada of *Impressions of Hume* (2005) and author of *Projection and Realism in Hume's Philosophy* (2007).

T0382054

CAMBRIDGE INTRODUCTIONS TO KEY
PHILOSOPHICAL TEXTS

This series offers introductory textbooks on what are considered to be the most important texts of Western philosophy. Each book guides the reader through the main themes and arguments of the work in question, while also paying attention to its historical context and its philosophical legacy. No philosophical background knowledge is assumed, and the books will be well suited to introductory university-level courses.

Titles published in the series:

BERKELEY'S *A TREATISE CONCERNING THE PRINCIPLES OF HUMAN KNOWLEDGE*

An Introduction

P. J. E. KAIL

University of Oxford

CAMBRIDGE
UNIVERSITY PRESS

CAMBRIDGE
UNIVERSITY PRESS

Shaftesbury Road, Cambridge CB2 8EA, United Kingdom

One Liberty Plaza, 20th Floor, New York, NY 10006, USA

477 Williamstown Road, Port Melbourne, VIC 3207, Australia

314–321, 3rd Floor, Plot 3, Splendor Forum, Jasola District Centre, New Delhi – 110025, India

103 Penang Road, #05–06/07, Visioncrest Commercial, Singapore 238467

Cambridge University Press is part of Cambridge University Press & Assessment, a department of the University of Cambridge.

We share the University's mission to contribute to society through the pursuit of education, learning and research at the highest international levels of excellence.

www.cambridge.org
Information on this title: www.cambridge.org/9780521173117

© P. J. E. Kail 2014

First published 2014

A catalogue record for this publication is available from the British Library

ISBN   978-1-107-00178-7   Hardback
ISBN   978-0-521-17311-7   Paperback

For Teddy
and my students, past, present and future
Sometimes ideal, and
never immaterial

Contents

Acknowledgements

The book was written with the support of the Master and Fellows of St Peter's College, Oxford, the Faculty of Philosophy, Oxford, and the wonderfully convivial Newberry Library in Chicago. Thanks to Hilary Gaskin and Gillian Dadd at Cambridge University Press, and Nicole Osbourne who had the difficult task of proofreading a version of this book. Thanks also to Lyn Flight for copy-editing and Carly Minsky for preparing the index.

A number of different people read parts of the manuscript at various stages. Thanks then to Arif Ahmed, Tim Mawson, Alasdair Richmond and Tom Stoneham. Among my students, particular thanks go to Sophia Nayak-Oliver, Oliver Sieweke and Joshua Wilce.

Thanks, of a different kind, to S. M. S. Pearsall and E. M. P. Kail.

CHAPTER I

Introduction

I BIOGRAPHICAL NOTE

George Berkeley was born in Kilkenny, Ireland, on 12 March 1685. He went up to Trinity College Dublin in 1700, and studied mathematics, classics, logic and philosophy, graduating in 1704. Between graduating and attaining a Fellowship in 1707, he wrote on mathematics and began developing the doctrine for which he is most famous, namely, his doctrine of immaterialism. In 1709, he published *An Essay Towards a New Theory of Vision*. This work develops a novel account of visual perception, which, though independent from Berkeley's immaterialism, nevertheless informs it. The work that is the focus of this book, *A Treatise Concerning the Principles of Human Knowledge*, was published in 1710, and a second edition, which differs in a number of ways, was published in 1734. The year 1712 saw the publication of *Passive Obedience*, a work that advocated the Christian doctrine that we must assent to the absolute supremacy of the Crown. In 1713, Berkeley visited London for the first time. He fell in with Swift, Addison, Pope and Gay (among others), and published *Three Dialogues Between Hylas and Philonous* (second edition, 1734) before his first brief tour of Continental Europe. A second continental trip in 1713, when he acted as tutor for St George Ashe, supposedly involved an attempt to meet the elderly Nicolas Malebranche in Paris before a longer stay in Italy. It is not known whether the two actually met. On his return from Europe he published an important essay on the philosophy of science, *De Motu* (*On Motion*) in 1721.

After a brief sojourn in London, Berkeley returned to Dublin and took the degrees of Bachelor of Divinity and Doctor of Divinity. He

was appointed Dean of Derry in 1724. Before this he was formulating
a scheme to found a missionary and arts college in Bermuda. He
crossed the Atlantic with his new bride Anne (née Forster), landing in
Virginia, and travelled from there to Rhode Island, where he built a
house, Whitehall, which still stands. The name took on an ironic
edge, since the money approved by Parliament for the college was
subsequently withheld, and Berkeley was forced to leave America and
go to London. His time, however, was not completely wasted, for
during it he wrote *Alciphron; or the Minute Philosopher*. The work was
a critique of non-Christian philosophers, or 'freethinkers', like
Mandeville and Shaftesbury, and it also illuminates a number of
aspects of Berkeley's thought, especially his views on language.

He was appointed bishop of Cloyne in 1734. In his later years, he
became very interested in the health benefits of tar water, a mixture of
pine tar and water in which the water was removed once the mixture
had settled. His most widely read work, *Siris: A Chain of Philosophical
Reflexions and Inquiries concerning the Virtues of Tar-water, and divers
other subjects* (1744), owed its success to his views on public health. Its
subjects are diverse: as well as the virtues of tar water – which Berkeley
also advocated in a number of magazine articles – the work discusses,
among other things, Platonism, immaterialism and the Trinity, and is
a philosophically fascinating text. Berkeley spent the last year of his
life in Holywell Street, Oxford, while his son George was attending
the university. He died on 14 January 1753, and, in a final ironic twist,
he is buried under the very solid material substance of the chapel of
John Locke's former college, Christ Church.

2 PRELIMINARIES AND OUTLINE

A Treatise Concerning the Principles of Human Knowledge, Part 1
(PHK) is a compact and brilliant piece, beautifully written, lucid,
and without a single redundant sentence. It comprises 156 numbered
sections, an introduction of 25 sections, a dedication, and a preface
(which was omitted from the second edition). In this section I shall
sketch the main threads of the work. The section also serves as an
outline of the present book since it follows, though with some
important deviations noted below, the order of the PHK. Before
sketching this outline some further remarks are necessary.

The full title of the PHK is *A Treatise Concerning the Principles of Human Knowledge, Part I*. But why 'Part I'? Or, more pointedly, where is Part II? One of Berkeley's correspondents, Samuel Johnson, wrote to him that he 'shall live with some impatience till I see the second part of your design accomplished'.[1] Berkeley replied that some fourteen years earlier he had lost the manuscript for Part II, upon which he had 'made a considerable progress', but 'never had the leisure since to do so disagreeable a thing as writing twice on the same subject'.[2] It is tempting to speculate that Berkeley did not really finish Part II and not for the reasons he mentions, not least because he certainly *did* have the leisure and he *does* write upon the same subject twice (the *Three Dialogues* covers much of the same ground as the PHK). Part II was most likely to be his account of spirits, including God, and of human action,[3] but, as we shall see in Chapter 8, there are some deep problems in Berkeley's account of spirits. Perhaps Berkeley found no satisfactory solution to those problems and simply abandoned Part II.[4] Whatever truth there may be in this speculation, the fact remains that there is no Part II.[5] However, as already indicated, Berkeley wrote more than just the PHK, and some of these other writings, if used carefully, are valuable sources of illumination. Most importantly, we have the aforementioned *Three Dialogues between Hylas and Philonous* (DHP).[6] The reception of the PHK was not as Berkeley had hoped, and so, writing on the same subject twice, he presented his immaterialist philosophy in a way he hoped was more digestible. It would, however, be a grave mistake to think that this work is nothing but a more popular repackaging of the PHK. It not only amplifies and clarifies the doctrines of the PHK, but also differs in some of its key claims, reflecting the fact that Berkeley was

---

[1] Johnson to Berkeley, 10 September 1729, in A. A. Luce and T. E. Jessop (eds), *The Works of George Berkeley, Bishop of Cloyne* (London: Thomas Nelson, 1949), vol. 2, p. 277.

[2] Berkeley to Johnson, 25 November 1729, *Works*, vol. 2, p. 282

[3] 'The 2 great Principles of Morality. The Being of a God & the Freedom of Man: these to be handled in the beginning of the Second Book', *Philosophical Commentaries* (PC), 508.

[4] For something like this suggestion, see Charles McCracken, 'Berkeley's Notion of Spirit', in M. Atherton (ed.), *The Empiricists: Critical Essays on Locke, Berkeley and Hume* (Lanham, MD: Rowman & Littlefield, 1999), pp. 145–52.

[5] In entry 585 Berkeley mentions a '3d book'.

[6] The character's names are revealing – they are derived from ancient Greek and Hylas is roughly translatable as 'matter'; Philonous, 'lover of spirit' or 'lover of mind'.

continuing to think about his philosophy. Indeed, Berkeley continued to think about the contents of both works, making some alterations when both went into second editions; we shall note some of these alterations during the course of this book. I shall make use of the *Dialogues* in many places, and quite extensively in Chapters 6 and 8.

As well as the *Dialogues*, we have what have become known as his *Philosophical Commentaries* (PC), two notebooks that record Berkeley's thoughts when he was working on *An Essay towards New Theory of Vision* and the PHK.[7] These must be used with care. The obvious reason to be careful when using them is that while writings that are published bear the imprimatur of the author's approval,[8] notebooks, never intended for publication, do not. Notebooks can contain many things, including records of thoughts subsequently abandoned – either because the author could not refine certain thoughts enough to let them see the light of day or because he or she came to believe the opposite. As we shall briefly see in Chapter 8, Berkeley changes his mind in the course of the notebooks themselves. So, when I use the notebooks I shall generally give priority to the published works and use material from them only when they illuminate the published claims. The same applies to the long draft introduction to the *Principles* that we have and to which I shall refer in Chapter 3. I shall also make some small use of *Alciphron* and *De Motu*, as well as both *An Essay toward a New Theory of Vision* and *The Theory of Vision Vindicated and Explained*.

Having spoken briefly about some of Berkeley's other works, it should be emphasised that this book is about Berkeley's *Principles* and *not* about his philosophy as a whole. I do not discuss many other aspects of Berkeley's thought, including his moral philosophy, his philosophy of money or his later Platonism in *Siris*. And although I shall briefly discuss aspects of his philosophy of science and his philosophy of mathematics in Chapter 7, these discussions are not intended to count as complete accounts of either topic. His views on both developed significantly from the early claims of the *Principles*,

---

[7] For a discussion of the notebooks, see Robert McKim, 'Berkeley's Notebooks', in K. Winkler (ed.), *The Cambridge Companion to Berkeley* (Cambridge University Press, 2005), pp. 63–93.
[8] Of course, an author can always come to regret and even disown something published under her or his own name.

and I have given the reader some references should they wish to follow the development of his thought. I shall also inform the reader when a particular claim is controversial, exegetically speaking. The interpretation of any philosophical text is a difficult matter and students are often surprised to learn just how divided scholars are, even on issues that might seem fairly fundamental. No doubt Berkeley scholars will find some of the claims in this book controversial, though it should be added that none of the controversial claims is peculiar to me. Needless to say, scholars will find these claims defended with insufficient scholarly rigour. The intention, however, is to convey to the reader some of the complexity involved in understanding Berkeley, rather than resolve these claims within the confines of an introductory book.

A final point before we turn to give an overview of the work. Student readers sometimes come to Berkeley with one or both of the following prejudices. Berkeley was a bishop and God plays a substantial role in his philosophy. If one is unsympathetic to such things one might write the system off as mere Christian apologetics. There is no doubt that Berkeley's philosophy is congenial to religion, and he writes that the *Principles* would be 'ineffectual, if by what I have said I cannot inspire my readers with a pious sense of the presence of God' (PHK §156). But Berkeley provides arguments for his position and the reader should engage with those arguments on their own terms.

The second prejudice, or perhaps preconception, concerns the central idea of Berkeley's philosophy. After five sections of the main text of the PHK Berkeley writes:

all the choir of heaven and furniture of the earth, in a word all those bodies which compose the mighty frame of the world, have not any subsistence without a mind … [and] consequently so long as they are not actually perceived by me … they must either have no existence at all, or else subsist in the mind of some eternal spirit. (PHK §6)

Physical things exist only when perceived either by some human person or by God.[9] This is the central thesis of his *immaterialism*.

---

[9] This disjunctive formulation (either things exist when perceived by some human or by God) is intended to reflect some deep complications in Berkeley's thought. For more on this, see Chapter 6.

The thesis is also commonly known as 'idealism', since physical objects are composed of 'ideas'. The lexicographer Samuel Johnson is famously reported to have kicked a large stone and at the same time declaimed 'I refute it thus!', and this reaction instances the second prejudice I have in mind, namely, that Berkeley's philosophy is just too bizarre to be taken seriously at all. However, it takes a good deal of care and thought to understand what is meant by claims such as the 'being' of tables and chairs 'is to be perceived or known' (PHK §6), and so any initial reaction is most likely to be extremely superficial. The reader should put any such superficial reaction to one side. Berkeley himself is clearly aware of the danger of a superficial reaction to his philosophy. He does not mention the central immaterialist claim of the mind-dependency of the world in the work's title, Introduction or its subtitle. The omission of any reference to imma-terialism is deliberate. Berkeley tells a friend in a letter that he intends that 'the notion might steal unawares on the reader, who possibly would never have meddled with a book that he had known contained such paradoxes'.[10] The preface to the first edition of the PHK implores the reader to 'suspend his judgement' until 'he has once, *at least*, read the whole through with that degree of attention and thought which the subject matter shall seem to deserve'. He is well aware that there are passages that, when taken in isolation, are 'very liable to gross misinterpretation, and to be charged with most absurd consequences'. Without careful consideration, the 'reader will be among those who are too apt to condemn an opinion before they right comprehend it'. Berkeley's advice to his readers is sound, and, indeed, applies to any philosophical position. It is always a mistake simply to react merely to the *conclusion* of any philosophical position, independently of the arguments advanced in favour of it. For although Berkeley tells us that the 'being' of an object like a chair is to be 'perceived or known', quite what that *means* is not something that can be properly understood without first understanding the arguments that support it. Indeed, Berkeley's *Dialogues* enacts this very point. Berkeley has Hylas remark early on that he had heard that Philonous, Berkeley's spokesman, is someone 'who maintained the most extravagant opinion that ever entered into the mind of man'

---

[10] Berkeley to Percival, 6 September 1710, *Works*, vol. 2, p. 36.

(DHP1 172).[11] This, Hylas has heard, 'in last night's conversation'. The remainder of the work sees Philonous engage Hylas in such a way that he comes to understand the central claim of immaterialism through an appreciation of the reasons behind it, rather than having it presented as a bald statement made for an evening's entertainment. So while at the beginning of the conversation Hylas' partial grasp of immaterialism led him to condemn it as a 'manifest piece of scepticism' (DHP1 172), he later recognises that although Philonous 'set out upon the same principles [of the sceptical] Academics,[12] Cartesians, and the like sects', his 'conclusions are directly opposite to theirs' (DHP3 262).

Fully grasping what the claim that the physical world depends on being perceived by spirits for its existence means, what its ramifications are, and how it fits into Berkeley's wider system, requires, then, careful study and thought. But we can begin to approach the meaning of immaterialism by simultaneously sketching the outline of the *Principles* and the present volume. According to its subtitle, the PHK examines 'the Chief Causes of Error and Difficulty in the *Sciences*, with the grounds of Scepticism, Atheism, and Irreligion, are inquired into'. This claim is not mere subterfuge, a thin cover for Berkeley's immaterialism. Berkeley is genuinely concerned with these issues and thinks that a key source of error, difficulty, scepticism, atheism and irreligion is the philosophical doctrine of *material substance*. Put crudely, materialism is the general thesis that the non-mental world is composed of extended unthinking material substance or substances whose existence does not depend on our perceiving it.[13] This thesis can be understood in different ways, and has different ramifications according to the varying stances of the particular philosophies that articulate it. Indeed, there was some profound disagreement about material substance, its powers and nature, and how and whether we can know its nature. Despite these differences, Berkeley saw the doctrine of material substance as the source of serious confusion,

---

[11] Page references are to Luce and Jessop, *Works*, but most modern editions have these page numbers in the margin for standard reference.
[12] 'Academics' here refers to a certain ancient school of scepticism.
[13] The word 'materialism' is often associated with the claim that the mind is material, but this is not what is meant in this context. Rather, a 'materialist' here simply means anyone who believes in the existence of material substance.

scepticism, danger to irreligion and an impediment to science. To understand Berkeley's immaterialism, then, we need to situate him in this context and that is the aim of Chapter 2, which provides a sketch of the key claims of two thinkers who both articulate versions of materialism and with whom Berkeley was deeply engaged, namely, Locke (1632–1704) and Nicolas Malebranche (1638–1715). I give a sketch of various themes that emerge from their respective philosophies and how, in outline, Berkeley's philosophy is a reaction to them.

*Im*materialism involves at least a rejection of *materialism*. Given this, one might think that Berkeley would open the *Principles* with an assault on materialism. But he does not. The *Principles* actually opens with a relatively lengthy introduction, and this is the subject of Chapter 3. The Introduction is puzzling in a number of different ways. First, in its twenty-five carefully worked and numbered sections there is not a single hint of immaterialism. It is oddly an introduction that makes no mention of the key claim of the work it introduces. Its contents include the nature and sources of scepticism, a criticism of the doctrine of 'abstract ideas' and a discussion of the different functions of language. The discussion of abstract ideas is targeted against Locke's account of how human beings acquire the capacity to think in general terms (for example, think of human beings in general) given that we perceive only particulars (this human or that one). This discussion is interesting but has a puzzling aspect. At PHK §4, Berkeley states that the opinion that physical things exist independently of the mind 'at bottom' depends on the doctrine of abstract ideas. But how could this be so? How could the view that objects exist independently of the mind depend on a philosophical theory of general thought? What is the dependence supposed to be? This question cannot be answered properly until Chapter 5, when we consider Berkeley's attacks on materialism.

We noted that Berkeley's *Principles* does not begin with an assault on materialism. One might find that puzzling if one thought that his case for immaterialism simply consists in a rejection of materialism. But this is a mistake. Berkeley has a positive argument *for* the claim that the world is mind-dependent, one that does not trade on showing that there is something faulty with materialism. His case for the central thesis of immaterialism in the PHK is exceedingly swift, comprising only six or so sections of the main text. This argument is the topic of Chapter 4. At a first approximation, the argument is as follows. Tables, chairs and all other physical objects are sensible objects. A sensible object is any object that is immediately perceived by sense. But what we perceive immediately by sense are mind-dependent *ideas*. So physical objects are mind-dependent. Crucial to understanding all this are the notions of *sensible object, immediate perception, idea* and *mind-dependence*. Chapter 4 discusses these key notions and identifies two interpretations of mind-dependence. One interpretation has Berkeley reducing the world to a collection of sensations akin to pain, private to each individual mind. The other interpretation views objects as exhausted by forms of *appearance*, and mind-dependent in the sense they exist only when there is some mind to which they appear. But they are not 'private' objects existing in particular minds. It is this that Berkeley means by his famous claim that the 'being' of a sensible object is 'to be perceived'. Any sensible object cannot be conceived as existing except in terms of its appearing *to* some mind, and it is this that makes for the mind-dependence of the physical world. These two interpretations are rather different, require some teasing out, and they condition how we understand the rest of the *Principles*. It is the second of these interpretations which is favoured in this work.

As I said above, Berkeley's case for immaterialism is not simply a matter of rejecting materialism, but it is certainly true that he wheels out a battery of arguments against various versions of it. These arguments are the subject of Chapter 5. Once materialism is despatched, we seem to be left only with ideas and minds, a position that seems far from our ordinary sense of the world and our place within it. The *Principles* now takes a constructive turn, rebuilding the world from these minimal materials. This rebuilding is the topic of Chapter 6. Central to Berkeley's reconstruction is God, who sustains the world in which we live. In the *Principles* the argument for the existence of God and Berkeley's God-based account of reality takes up only a small number of passages (PHK §§25–33), but there are many complexities lying behind this brisk progression. In order to illuminate Berkeley's account of reality, therefore, I shall bring in some quite substantial material from the *Three Dialogues*. This material helps with a number of issues. One such issue is that of understanding the character of Berkeley's argument for the existence of God. A second is whether Berkeley holds that sensible objects *continue* to exist when unperceived by any particular human being. This issue emerges from one of many objections Berkeley considers to his system in §§34–84 of the *Principles*. How can an object continue to exist when I do not perceive it if its existence is perception-dependent? In the *Principles*, Berkeley allows that it is possible that sensible objects continue to exist unperceived by me and you, whereas in the *Dialogues* not only does he grant it possible, but he commits himself to the claim that they *do* so exist. Understanding Berkeley's thought here reveals a great deal about how we are to understand some central notions in his philosophy, including mind-dependence, the nature of reality and the role of God.

In Chapter 7 we consider some more of the objections to his system that Berkeley mentions, this time those concerning the compatibility, or otherwise, of immaterialism with the practice of science. When rebuilding the world from minds and ideas, Berkeley exploits the claim that all ideas are completely inert and are brought into existence or changed by spirits. Real things are ideas caused by the spirit that is God, imaginary things are ideas caused by finite spirits, namely, us. This implies that the things composing reality are entirely passive. This offends both common sense and science. It offends common sense because we think that things in the world are related by cause and effect. We think fire burns and diamonds scratch glass. It offends science, since science appears to be in the business of explaining natural events by locating fundamental relations of cause and effect. Berkeley's answer to these objections ultimately rests on a very distinctive claim. The relations between worldly things we take to be relations of cause and effect are relations of *sign* and *signified*. The world we mistakenly take to be causally structured is semantically structured. It is a language through which God communicates to us, and which science and, ultimately, philosophy seek to interpret. Understanding the world is not explanation but interpretation. Berkeley not only takes his philosophy to meet the objections, but also to be positively advantageous to science, a claim he expounds at PHK §§101–17. He thinks, furthermore, that his philosophy is equally advantageous to arithmetic and geometry (PHK §§118–34). Chapter 7, therefore, also charts the main contours of these sections.

The remaining sections of the *Principles* concern spirits, both finite spirits and the infinite spirit of God. Its explicit concerns are how we know our own spirit or mind, how we know that there are other finite minds, and how we know that there is the infinite mind of God. Berkeley thinks his system shows that we have overwhelming evidence for this existence of God and we 'may . . . assert, that the existence of God is far more evidently perceived than the existence of men' (PHK §147). But Berkeley is optimistic here, to say the least, for there are two fundamental issues in his account of spirit that his works do not adequately discuss. The first is what kind of thing a spirit is supposed to be. As we shall see, this is an exceedingly difficult and controversial matter. The second issue is how we know spirits in our own case. How, that is, we each of us know we are a spirit. Again, this is a very thorny issue for Berkeley. In addressing both these issues we depart from the *Principles* and seek illumination in other texts, though I shall suggest, in the end, that we do not get very far. Finally, we turn to another problem for Berkeley's spirits, how spirits can act in a world where real things are those that are caused by God.

CHAPTER 2

Context and aims

I THE SUBTITLE TO THE *PRINCIPLES* AND TWO
INTERLOCUTORS

Berkeley's *Principles*, and the immaterialist philosophy it embodies, has a number of definite aims. The general tenor of them is evident from its subtitle, which, as we noted, is 'wherein the Chief Causes of Error and Difficulty in the *Sciences*, with the grounds of Scepticism, Atheism, and Irreligion, are inquired into'. Berkeley sees the dangers of scepticism, atheism and irreligion as stemming from philosophical sources, rather than a threat stemming from ordinary common sense.[1] The philosophy with which he is concerned is the then relatively new 'mechanical philosophy', an immensely subtle and complex world view associated with the 'scientific revolution', the crowning achievement of which was the work of Isaac Newton.

A pioneer in this new philosophy was René Descartes (1596–1650). For him, the ultimate nature of the material world is knowable to humans and it consists of extended things in motion. All else that we seem to perceive – colours, tastes, smells, etc. – are best understood in terms of the effects of matter in motion on minds. As Richard Westfall puts it in a now classic study 'bodies comprise only particles of matter in motion, and all their apparent qualities (extension alone excluded) are merely sensations excited by bodies in motion . . . The world is a machine, composed of inert bodies, moved by physical necessity, indifferent to the existence of thinking beings.'[2] This austere view of the world was driven by a new conception of science, which, very

---

[1] Compare Chapter 3, section 2, pp. 36–38.
[2] Richard S. Westfall, *The Construction of Modern Science: Mechanisms and Mechanics* (Cambridge University Press, 1971), p. 33.

roughly, aspired to explain the behaviour of the physical world by appealing to as few a number of properties as possible. Descartes contrasts this aspiration with 'scholastic philosophy', which he is keen to reject as explanatorily bankrupt in its constant appeal to numerous 'qualities' or 'forms' to 'explain' observable phenomena, themselves stand in need of explanation. Thus, he writes:

> If you find it strange that ... I do not use the qualities called 'heat', 'cold', 'moisture' and 'dryness' – as the [scholastic] philosophers do – I shall say to you that these qualities themselves seem to need explanation ... not only these four qualities, but all the others as well, including even the forms of inanimate matter, can be explained without the need to suppose in the matter other than the motion, size, shape and arrangements of its parts.[3]

Though optimistic Descartes was at the same time aware of the problems and limitations of this new world view, and much subsequent thought grappled with them. A torrent of intellectual water passed under the bridge between Descartes and Berkeley in the effort to think through mechanism, and with it crashing waves of dispute and the emergence of distinct intellectual tributaries. To get some sense of the state of play in philosophy that informs Berkeley's thought, and the aspects of it he took to be conducive to scepticism, irreligion, atheism, and the errors and difficulties in the sciences, we shall not go far wrong if we consider the thought of John Locke, Nicolas Malebranche and, to a lesser extent, Descartes himself. Locke and Malebranche published massive and widely studied masterpieces within a few years of each other: Locke's *An Essay Concerning Human Understanding*, first published in 1689; and Malebranche's *De la recherche de la vérité* (*The Search After Truth*), first published 1674–5. Both works concern the methods of sciences, the perceptual and cognitive faculties of the human mind, and the nature, status and limitations of the mechanical philosophy. It is Locke and Malebranche with whom Berkeley grapples most in the *Commentaries*. It would be absurd to think that this pair constitute the whole of the mechanical philosophy or, indeed, that they were the only two philosophers with whom Berkeley was concerned. Newton

---

[3] From *The World*, in John Cottingham, Robert Stoothoff and Dugald Murdoch, *The Philosophical Writings of Descartes*, 2 vols. (Cambridge University Press, 1985), vol. 1, p. 89. Henceforth: CSM.

was also never far from Berkeley's mind, as we shall in Chapter 7. But it is undeniable that these two figures greatly animated him. He by no means found each and every aspect of Locke and Malebranche objectionable. Locke and Malebranche disagree profoundly on a number of issues, and Berkeley agreed on this with Locke and on that with Malebranche, while he also rejected, absorbed and transformed elements of their thinking; his relation to them is neither pure rejection nor passive acceptance. Furthermore, Berkeley's brilliance cannot be reduced to a mere synthesis of these two philosophies.[4] Nevertheless, it is these thinkers that represent the greatest threat of scepticism, atheism and error, and Berkeley is thoroughly engaged with both of them. Sketching this thought and Berkeley's reaction to it greatly illuminates Berkeley's thought.

2 IDEAS AND INTELLECT

A first and fundamental issue during this period was that of how the human mind could be capable of thought and representation. Agreed on all hands is that in order to think of anything we must have an *idea* of that thing. But what *are* ideas? And how do they represent? In this connection, Berkeley is customarily classified as an 'empiricist', one of the great trio of Locke, Berkeley and Hume.[5] An empiricist holds that all representation is derived from, and is constrained by, experience. For Locke, all our ideas are derived from sensory experience or experience of the operation of our own minds ('ideas of reflection'). The basic intuition at play here is that we cannot *think* about something unless we first have seen, felt, heard, tasted, touched or been aware of it occurring in one's own mind. Thinking is centrally a matter of having mental *images*, derived from experiences, and such images *represent* their objects in virtue of *resembling* them. My idea of square is an image of a square and it represents, or is about, a square

---

[4] So I am not, by situating Berkeley against this background, claiming that all his thinking is reducible to a combination or synthesis of Cartesian and Lockean sources. For scepticism on viewing Berkeley in this way, see Stephen H. Daniel, 'How Berkeley's Works are Interpreted', in S. Parigi (ed.), *George Berkeley: Religion and Science in the Age of Enlightenment* (Dordrecht: Springer, 2010), pp. 3–14.

[5] For a critical discussion of Berkeley as an empiricist, see M. R. Ayers, 'Was Berkeley an Empiricist or a Rationalist?', in K. Winkler (ed.), *The Cambridge Companion to Berkeley* (Cambridge University Press, 2005), pp. 34–62.

because it resembles a square. This idea of representation as resemblance is something we shall expand on in section 5 below, but the main point to note at this stage is that all mental operations are a matter of manipulating these images. For example, new ideas or representations can be constructed by combining those derived from experience. I can come to have the thought of a unicorn by combining my image of a horn with an image of a horse. This conception of the *origins* of our thought is linked to a view of its *constraints*. What I can think is limited to my ideas, and since all ideas are derived from sensation and reflection, any thought I can have must somehow relate to these materials. One might combine ideas of what one has encountered in experience to make a new idea of what one has not in the manner mentioned above, but my being able to do so requires that what I combine are materials encountered in experience. But if we cannot relate a putative thought to sense experience, then the putative thought is no thought at all. This point connects to what Locke has to say about language. He has much to say about the way in which ideas relate to language, and devotes a whole book of *An Essay Concerning Human Understanding*, entitled 'Of Words', to the topic. What is it that makes the noises or marks that are words significant? Words have meaning or signification in virtue of their being attached to ideas, so the 'aboutness' of words is derived from the fact that *ideas* represent things. The *function* of words is to 'stand for' these ideas and, furthermore, convey or communicate ideas to others. If there is no idea appropriately related to a given word, then that word lacks a meaning and is insignificant.

The empiricists are customarily contrasted with the 'rationalist' group of Descartes, Malebranche, Spinoza and Leibniz. This is a line that is controversial to scholars, but one way to draw it turns on the nature of ideas, which in turn has deep ramifications for the extent and nature of our capacity to represent the world and, in particular, material substance. For the rationalist, although it is true that we often employ sensory materials in thought, our capacity to form thoughts of the world is *not* constrained by what is provided by the senses. We have additionally the capacity to form non-sensory *intellectual* representations. One thing that non-sensory or intellectual representations enable the mind to do is to grasp the nature of the material world that lies beyond experience. This is something we shall take up in the next section. Another reason offered in support of the intellect is that while we only perceive particular things in sense experience, our thoughts can be about things in general. I can think of tigers in general, as opposed to some particular tiger, and I can think of redness rather than particular red patches. To account for that we must have a capacity that goes beyond simply the particulars given in sense experience; Malebranche and the other rationalists think we must have ideas of the intellect that are themselves inherently general. Our non-sensory idea of extension is of extension *in general* rather than of this or that particular extension. In Malebranche's peculiar take on the claim, these general intellectual ideas are entities in the mind of God to which our minds are directed. This is his celebrated (or notorious) 'vision in God' doctrine. God has ideas that are inherently representational entities and serve as the general archetypes or blueprints for the created world. Our minds represent because our minds are related to abstract objects or ideas. To the extent to which we engage our pure intellect, our minds are in an intimate relation with the mind of God and 'the mind can see God's works in Him, provided that God wills to reveal it'.[6] We 'see' His ideas, platonic archetypes in His mind, and these ideas are objects of our intellect, constituting 'the intelligible world or the place of minds'.[7] This account of the nature of the ideas and the intellect was extremely controversial during the period, but nevertheless there was agreement from many philosophers that we do have such non-sensory representations, though more typically rationalists held that such inherently general ideas are innate. We are born with the capacity to represent the general.

Locke disagreed on a number of counts. Not only does he hold that there are only ideas derived from experience, he also eschews general entities (there is no 'extension itself'). There exist only the particular things we encounter in ordinary experience. Furthermore, no idea is innate. Nevertheless, we can think of extension in general, or redness rather than particular instances of red. But how? Locke's answer is that we can form *abstract ideas* by considering the particulars

[6] Nicolas Malebranche, *The Search After Truth*, trans. Thomas Lennon and Paul Olscamp (Cambridge University Press, 1997), p. 230. Henceforth: *Search*.

[7] *Search*, p. 235.

that we have encountered in experience and 'abstracting' from them. So having encountered several particular cats, I (somehow) abstract away from these particular instances, therefore equipping myself with the capacity to think about cats in general without any need for the intellect.

This is something we shall examine in more detail in Chapter 3. Now, with one notorious exception,[8] Berkeley holds – with Locke – that thinking or representing involves ideas that are sensory in nature: 'Pure Intellect I understand not' (PC 810).[9] In rejecting the intellect Berkeley, like Locke, also rejects the intellectualist conception of general thought and its objects. But he is dead set against Locke's account of abstraction. There cannot be abstract *ideas* in the way that Locke construes them. This is not merely an issue in philosophy of mind and language, however (though it is that too). Berkeley claims that the 'doctrine of abstraction [is] of very evil consequence in the all the Sciences' (PC 564). Just why this is so is taken up in various places in this book.[10] Berkeley also rejects Locke's views about the function of language. Language is more than merely the communication of ideas, and Locke's mistake leads him into the error of supposing material substance.[11]

3 MATERIAL SUBSTANCE AND A FIRST SOURCE OF SCEPTICISM

So far throughout this book I have written indifferently about 'physical' or 'material' objects like tables or chairs, etc., relying on an intuitive notion of the things we encounter in everyday life. We think that such objects exist independently of our own or anyone else's perception of them.[12] The doctrine of 'material substance' is a philosophical thesis that goes beyond such a claim by offering a metaphysical-*cum*-scientific *interpretation* of material objects, and, as

---

[8] This exception is discussed in Chapter 8.
[9] Compare PC 779. Berkeley nevertheless holds that God's ideas are intellectual. This fact is connected with a problem regarding how to understand the relation between our ideas and God's, see Chapter 6, section 3, pp. 93–98.
[10] See Chapter 3, Chapter 5, section 5, pp. 79–82, Chapter 6, section 6, p. 106, and Chapter 7, section 4, pp. 102–131.
[11] See Chapter 3, section 5, pp. 49–53, and Chapter 5, section 5, pp. 79–82.
[12] Berkeley argues that we do not really think this. See Chapter 5, section 3, pp. 79–82.

we shall see, Berkeley holds that this interpretation of ordinary thought is a fundamentally incorrect one. It is a mistaken philosophical view imposed upon ordinary thought, distorting its innocent commitments.

One key metaphysical component of this distorting picture is the notion of *substancehood*. The topic of substance is one of the dominant themes of early modern philosophy, and discussions of it are subtle, complex and, at times, bewildering, but a general outline will suffice here.[13] The intuition behind the notion of a substance is that there is a fundamental distinction between qualities and properties, on the one hand, and the things that 'own' or 'possess' those qualities, on the other. Substances are those things the existence of which does not depend on anything else. Modes or attributes depend on substances for their existence.[14] The *identity* of any particular individual is determined by its being a substance. A single thing can have many different dependent qualities at a particular time, but those different qualities form a unity by being qualities or modes of a single substance (this is called 'synchronic' identity). An individual can remain numerically the same thing through changes in its qualities because the same substance remains through those changes (this is called 'diachronic' identity). So the statue that was red remains the same statue when painted blue because the substance persists through this change in its quality. Substances fall into different *kinds*, and for the early modern period the discussion centred on two main kinds, material substance and mental substance. What makes any substance the kind of substance it is, is its *essence*, the property or properties that any substance cannot lose and yet remain the substance that it is. For example, Descartes held that the essential property – or principal attribute – of a mind or mental substance is *thought*, not this or that particular thought, but thought in general. Anything that thinks is a mental substance, and any non-thinking substance is not a mental substance.

---

[13] Roger Woolhouse, *Descartes, Spinoza, Leibniz: The Concept of Substance in Seventeenth-Century Metaphysics* (London: Routledge 1993), remains an extremely useful introduction.

[14] There is a complication here inasmuch as this world contains *created* substances that are in some sense dependent upon God for their existence. I shall ignore this complication, though I hope not in a way that gives the impression that matters were straightforward for the early moderns on this score.

How is this abstract philosophical apparatus applied to the material world? If matter is a substance, then we need to determine what its essence is, what its modes are, and the sense in which those modes depend on upon it. As mentioned above, Descartes and Malebranche thought that the intellect allowed us to know the nature of the material world perfectly. Descartes, in his *Meditations on First Philosophy*, tried to illustrate the intellect by asking the reader to consider a piece of wax, both before and after heat is applied to it by placing it by a fire. Before heat is applied, the wax smells and taste of honey from the hive from which it is taken, it is solid, cold, hard and sounds when struck. When placed near the fire, it melts, and all its 'sensible qualities' change. It becomes liquid, translucent, its smell and taste change, and yet, suggests Descartes, we know the wax 'distinctly' and yet its identity can be distinguished by 'none of the features which I arrived at by means of the senses' since these have changed.[15] What remains constant is that the wax is *extended*.

Extension is therefore the essence of matter. Anything that is a material object is extended in space, and there cannot be material objects without extension. All other material things are *modes* of extension. Being triangular is a mode of extension – a triangle is a dependent being – since there cannot be triangularity without extension. So we can grasp just what the essence of the world is and how modes like triangularity are dependent on extension. The 'knowledge we have of [body] is quite perfect', claims Malebranche.[16] We can understand transparently just how a particular mode of extension depends on its essence in a geometrical form. Through the intellect we can grasp that matter is essentially extension, and understand how its modes depend on it, and so we understand in principle just what the material world is and how its changes depend on its nature.

Locke's view is rather different from the Cartesians. Whilst he maintains the metaphysical framework of substance/mode, he certainly does not hold that matters are as transparent as the Cartesians think. The lack of an intellectual faculty is one thing that puts paid to Cartesian optimism. Locke, who holds that sensory experience is the only source of ideas, thinks that our grasp of matter is limited, and, at best, constitutes a conjecture reinforced by experimental

[15] CSM, vol. 2, p. 20.   [16] *Search*, p. 237.

study. Sensation and reflection exhaust the sources of ideas, so we must acknowledge 'how much these few and narrow Inlets are disproportionate to the vast whole Extent of all Beings'.[17] The '*ideas*, we can attain by our Faculties, are very disproportionate to Things themselves'.[18] On Locke's view, our natural faculties limit our understanding of the material world. We 'suppose' that there are substances that underwrite the regularities revealed by sense experience, but we have no idea of pure substance in general. We merely suppose an 'unknown support of qualities', where the 'true import of the Word [support], is in plain *English, standing under*, or *upholding*'.[19]

Locke thinks we have different ideas of different kinds of substances as well as material substance in general. We have ideas of kinds, like gold or water, differences reflected in the fact that our sensory ideas tend to be clustered in different ways. We associate a certain colour, texture, etc. under the term 'gold'. These groupings partly reflect our own interests and purposes. We categorise things into different kinds simply by noticing the regular ways in which qualities are connected. This grouping of ideas under terms like 'gold' or 'water' constitutes what Locke calls the *nominal* essence of kinds. But we also suppose that these differences reflect differences in which particles of matter are configured. These differences in configuration constitute the *real* essences of kinds. The real essence of gold is 'the constitution of the insensible parts of that Body, on which those [perceived] Qualities, and all the other Properties of *Gold* depend'.[20] These real essences of things are unknowable to us, Locke argues; ''Tis evident the internal constitution, whereon their Properties depend, is unknown to us.'[21]

Not only are we limited to the nominal essence of kinds of things, we are also limited to the nominal essence of matter itself. Descartes and Malebranche held that we know it is essentially extension, whereas Locke offers a nominal essence drawn from experience, which he thinks probably approximates its real essence. He holds that material substances share solidity, extension, figure, motion or

---

[17] E.4.3.22. References by book, chapter and section number, to P. H. Nidditch (ed.), *An Essay Concerning Human Understanding* (Oxford: Clarendon Press, 1975).
[18] E 4.3.22.   [19] E 2.23.3.   [20] E 3.6.2.   [21] E 3.6.9.

rest, and number. Anything that is a material object has these 'primary qualities', since it is these that are required to explain the behaviour of material objects. In addition to these primary qualities, our idea of matter includes its powers to affect other objects and to produce experiences in us (we shall look at these below). But whereas Descartes and Malebranche hold that we know the essence of matter and can understand fully material things, Locke counsels modesty. God has 'fitted our Senses, Faculties, and Organs, to the conveniences Life, and the Business we have to do here . . . But it appears not, that God intended, we should have a perfect, clear, and adequate Knowledge of [substances]; that perhaps is not the Comprehension of any finite being.'[22]

The fact that Berkeley sides with Locke in rejecting the intellect obviously puts him at a distance from Malebranche and Descartes. But the mixture of empiricism and the supposition of material substance in Locke is something that repels Berkeley. On Locke's view, the nature of the world is fundamentally closed to us. Locke views this as cognitive modesty. We have 'not much Reason to complain of the narrowness of our Minds, if we will but employ them about what may be of use to us' (E 1.1.5). Unlike Plato's sun, which illuminates our understanding, our source of light is akin to a candle 'that is set up for us, [and] shines bright enough for all our Purposes' (E 1.1.5). But where Locke saw modesty, Berkeley saw scepticism. 'We should believe', he writes, 'that God has dealt more bountifully with the sons of men, than to give them a strong desire for . . . knowledge, which he has placed quite out of their reach' (PHK 1 §3). Or, as he puts it in the Preface to the DHP, Locke's view contains 'scepticism and *paradox*. It is not enough, that we see and feel, that we taste and smell a thing. Its true nature, its absolute external entity, is still concealed.' Berkeley rejects the existence of material substance and removes the scepticism and paradox in one fell swoop. Indeed, not only does he reject material substance, he rejects the whole metaphysical apparatus of substance and mode when applied to the physical world. As we shall see, Berkeley thinks that, ultimately speaking, a physical thing is just a bundle or collection of qualities. The

---

[22] E 3.23.6.

problems of trying to understand just how qualities 'depend' on substances and what substances are simply disappears.[23]

There is a further problem relating to material substance or, rather, the relation between material substance and *mind*. How are the two kinds of substance related? For the Cartesians, just as the essence of matter is extension, the essence of mind is thought. These two substances are entirely different in kind, leading to a question with regard to how they interact. Descartes' answer is difficult to gauge, and in that respect is unsatisfactory, but Malebranche's answer is clear. There is no causal interaction between mind and matter. Instead, the relation between the two is secured by the only genuine power in the world, namely, God's will. This answer of Malebranche's is not simply an *ad hoc* and desperate response to a difficult question, but is instead a consequence of a general thesis that the only genuine power in the universe is God. We shall discuss this briefly below (section 6). Locke's response is again an appeal to the limits of understanding. We do not know the relation between thought and matter because we do not know enough about mental or material substance.[24] Again, Berkeley finds this unsatisfactory and removes the problem by removing material substance.

4 PERCEPTION AND A SECOND SOURCE OF SCEPTICISM

We are aware of material objects through sense perception. We see them, touch them, hear them and so on. But just what is it to perceive an object? This issue is a fundamental one – perhaps *the* fundamental one – for Berkeley. Looking at my watch right now, there is an object that is a certain shape, with texture and patterns of colours. So perhaps perceiving is a matter of direct awareness of (a certain range of) the object's properties. The watch, its colour, its shape, etc., are 'present to the mind', and the way the watch *seems* to me in experience is a matter of the watch *being* the way it seems. It looks grey, for example, because it is grey. This 'naive view' of perception holds that perceiving is a matter of a basic form of awareness of an object and its properties, a notion that cannot be understood in any simpler terms.

---

[23] See Chapter 5, section 4, pp. 77–79 and Chapter 6, section 6, pp. 104–107. Some commentators also see him as sceptical about whether the notion of substance and mode is applicable to minds. See Chapter 8, section 2, pp. 133–140.

[24] See also below, this chapter, section 7, p. 37.

Both Locke and Malebranche believe that this cannot be the correct view of our perceptual relation to physical objects. Our awareness of physical objects cannot be direct, but must be mediated by ideas. For Locke, all ideas are akin to bodily pains and tingles, a matter of raw feels of which we have immediate awareness and which give perceptual experience its distinct sensory or qualitative character.[25] It is these that are direct objects of awareness rather than physical objects. Consider, for example, your visual experience right now. It is of a page with black and white lines arranged in a particular way. On the Lockean picture what you are immediately aware of is not the page or the lines, but a visual experience that is composed of a certain structure of sensations. How then do we perceive physical objects? I become *indirectly* aware of the physical object when that object – the page – appropriately *causes* the idea of which I am directly aware. There are some complications with this picture that we shall consider in the next section, but what we have here is the essence of what is known as the 'representational' theory of perception. One perceives a material object by being aware of a mental object that represents the material one. It is also sometimes known as 'indirect realism'. 'Indirect' because physical objects are perceived indirectly through our direct awareness of ideas. 'Realism' because what we perceive, albeit indirectly, exists independently of our perception of it.

Malebranche's account of perception, though different in many ways from Locke's, is nevertheless also a form of indirect realism. He also took it that we have immediate awareness of ideas, rather than of physical objects, but these ideas are the abstract entities that are God's intellectual ideas. These are necessary to perceive objects because Malebranche held that the only items that are intrinsically representational – the only things that are *about* anything else – are God's ideas, and our capacity to perceive external objects is parasitic upon them. But if God's ideas are abstract forms, and we are directly aware of them, how do we perceive particular objects? This involves not merely the ideas of the intellect, but sensations, which God causes in the subject, which help to 'particularise' one's experience, making it about

---

[25] At least as he is standardly understood. The standard view is challenged by John Yolton in *John Locke and the Way of Ideas* (Oxford: Clarendon Press, 1956).

some particular object or another.[26] Berkeley thinks that indirect perception is not properly perception at all. To perceive something is to be in a direct and intimate relation to it, a matter of it being simply 'before the mind'.[27] Locke and Malebranche are distorting our ordinary, albeit implicit, view of the perceptual relation.[28]

Berkeley was also acutely aware that indirect perception opens up another space that the sceptic can inhabit. If what we are directly aware of is something non-physical, be it a sensory or an abstract idea in the mind of God, how do we know – if we do know – that there are physical objects that such experiences apparently represent? How do we know that there is anything 'beyond' ideas? This is a problem that Descartes raised (and thought he had answered) in the course of the investigation of his *Meditations*, a problem now known as 'Cartesian scepticism'. Descartes' proof that there is an external world appeals to God (a 'very unexpected circuit' as Hume would later tartly observe). We have a strong propensity to believe that there are such things and God would not deceive us in this regard.[29] Malebranche, for reasons we will not go into here, rejects this argument, and instead holds that our strong inclination rests on faith:[30] 'faith obliges us to believe that there are bodies ... [but] as for evidence, it seems to me that it is incomplete and that we are not invincibly led to believe there is something other than God and our own mind'.[31] Locke, by contrast, seems completely unmoved by the sceptical worry, claiming that while 'the Mind knows not Things immediately, but only by the intervention of the *Ideas* it has of them',[32] we nevertheless have 'sensitive knowledge' of the 'particular existence of finite beings without us'.[33]

---

[26] See, e.g., *Search*, Elucidation 10, p. 623 and *Dialogues Concerning Metaphysics and Religion*, trans. N. Jolley and D. Scott (Cambridge University Press, 2007), p. 17.

[27] See Chapter 4, section 3.

[28] Berkeley allows for a category of *mediate* perception, but this is not the same as the problematic *indirect* perception of Locke and Malebranche. For discussion, see Chapter 4, section 3.

[29] See the sixth *Meditation*.

[30] Locke himself noted this to be a danger in Malebranche's philosophy in his *An Examination of P. Malebranche's Opinion of Seeing All Things in God*, published posthumously in 1706.

[31] *Search*, 527   [32] E 4.4.3.

[33] E 4.2.14. For a discussion, see M. R. Ayers, *Locke* (London: Routledge 1991), vol. 1, Pt III.

Berkeley was singularly unimpressed with both Locke's and Malebranche's responses to this sceptical possibility. Malebranche did admit that the existence of bodies was doubtful (cf. PC 800), and, with Malebranche, Berkeley was unpersuaded that the fact that our sensory experience sometimes occurs independently of our will proves that there are material objects.[34] He felt that Locke simply failed to appreciate the problem. But the problem disappears when we get rid of the idea that there are two different things: immediately perceived ideas and physical objects. Chairs, tables, trees and other real things just *are* ideas that are immediately perceived. 'I am', writes Berkeley, 'farthest from Scepticism of any. man. I know with an intuitive knowledge of other things [besides his own existence]. this is w^r Locke nor scarce any other Thinking Philosopher will pretend to' (PC 563). Immanuel Kant would later claim that it was a 'scandal of philosophy' that we must accept the existence of external objects without proof. Berkeley's solution is straightforward. The scepticism is generated by exploiting what is only an imaginary gap between real things and our sense experience. Real things just *are* collections of ideas that are immediately perceived. There is, therefore, no gap between what we immediately perceive and the things that constitute reality.[35]

5 SECONDARY QUALITIES, MATTER AND OUR ORDINARY EXPERIENCE OF THE WORLD

The doctrine of material substance implies, though in different ways, that there is less to physical objects than meets the eye, the ear or any other sense. Recall that Malebranche held the essence of material objects to consist in extension, and that Locke held that the nominal essence of material substance includes extension, figure, motion or rest, number and solidity. Each philosopher took only these properties to be explanatory of the behaviour of physical objects. But we ordinarily attribute to physical objects a richer range of qualities. We attribute to objects colours, tastes, smells and other such qualities. Materialist philosophers therefore drew a distinction between two

---

[34] Berkeley credits this argument to Locke and Descartes at PC 790.
[35] See further Chapter 5, section 5, pp. 79–80.

classes of property attributed to material substance: *primary* and *secondary*. The former are the properties which our experience represents the objects to possess and which are necessary to explain the behaviour of the physical world, and the latter are qualities our experience represents objects to possess, but which are – depending on which particular version of the distinction is favoured – problematic in one way or another.[36]

Locke's discussion of this distinction is the most famous, so we shall begin with his account.[37] One key aspect of Locke's version of the distinction turns on whether or not our sensory ideas 'resemble' the qualities of the material objects that cause them in the minds of observers.[38] We mentioned above that ideas gain their representational qualities by resembling their causes. According to Locke, our ideas of primary qualities resemble the properties that cause them in us. My experience of a book is extended in my visual field and so is 'like' the extension of the book. The resemblance of idea and cause is what enables one's idea to serve as a representation of its object.[39] Lockean secondary qualities are those qualities that cause ideas in us that do *not* resemble their causes, but which we nevertheless 'imagine . . . are the resemblances of something, of something really existing in the Objects themselves', and include colour, taste and smell.[40] We imagine physical objects have something just 'like' the distinct qualitative experience of redness we enjoy when we open our eyes. But Locke holds that there is nothing like that idea possessed by material objects. Instead, there are certain arrangements of primary qualities – the light-reflecting textures of the surfaces of objects – that constitute a 'power' to produce such distinct ideas in us. The distinctive experience we associate with red is an effect of the powers of objects on our

---

[36] For an excellent survey see A. D. Smith, 'Of Primary and Secondary Qualities', *Philosophical Review* 99 (1990), 221–54.

[37] Locke also recognises 'tertiary qualities', the powers objects have in virtue of their primary qualities to affect other objects (E 2.8.23). Our idea of a physical object comprises its primary qualities and its powers.

[38] For a contemporary, and sympathetic, development of Lockean resemblance, see E. J. Lowe, 'Experience and its Objects', in T. Crane (ed.), *The Contents of Experience: Essays on Perception* (Cambridge University Press, 1992), pp. 79–104.

[39] This supposed relation of resemblance between ideas and physical qualities is something that Berkeley rejects. See Chapter 5, section 2.

[40] E 2.8.25.

sensory apparatus, just as the distinctive sensation of pain can be the effect of dropping something on one's feet. The only relevant difference is we suppose something like the experience or sensation is in the object in the former case and not the latter case.

Does this mean that objects do not have colours, or tastes or smells? Although Locke vacillates a little, he does not really deny that objects have colours. Instead, such qualities are identical to the particular arrangements of primary qualities or powers that produce the relevant ideas.[41] The fact that such ideas are the regular effects of these qualities is what makes them function as representations of those qualities, even if they do not resemble their causes. When we liberate ourselves from the mistaken supposition that there is something like our idea of red on the surfaces of objects, we assume that there is something that is its cause even if we cannot tell just what that is simply by looking, and we treat the idea as a *sign* for that unknown quality.[42]

Locke's version of the distinction has great affinities with Descartes'. One thing they share is the conviction that we do not really know, independent of scientific investigation, what the nature of redness is; we cannot tell on the basis of perception what redness really is. Non-scientists are really ignorant of what redness is, beyond saying that it is 'something' that causes the relevant sensation. Thus, in the 1644 *Principles of Philosophy* Descartes writes:

> It is clear, then, that when we say that we perceive colours in objects, this is really just the same as saying that we perceive something in the objects whose nature we do not know, but which produces in us a certain clear and very vivid sensation which we call the sensation of colour [and, furthermore] we do not really know what we are calling a colour.[43]

The joint claim that, say, (a) colours really are arrangements of primary qualities, and (b) we do not know pre-science, what, for example, redness is, is something that Malebranche subsequently criticised, and this criticism led to a different formulation of the primary/secondary quality distinction.[44] He emphasises that what

---

[41] There are complex issues lurking here regarding just how to understand the notion of 'power' and its relation to arrangements of primary qualities, but we can put these aside for our purposes.

[42] See Chapter 5, section 2.   [43] CSM, vol. 1, p. 218.

[44] For discussion, see Tad Schmaltz, 'Malebranche's Cartesianism and Lockean Colours', *History of Philosophy Quarterly*, 12 (1995), 387–403.

we ordinarily mean by 'colour' is not some unknown arrangement of primary qualities that causes sensations in us, but the sensuous qualities that Locke and Descartes think belong only to sensations. At best a term like colour is *equivocal*:

> If by heat, colour, flavour, you mean such and such a movement of insensible parts, then fire is hot, grass green, sugar sweet ... But if by heat and other qualities you mean what I feel near fire, what I see when I see grass ... then fire is not hot at all, nor is grass green ... for the heat we feel and the colours we see are only in the soul.[45]

Our ordinary conception of colour and other sensible qualities clashes with the claims of mechanical sciences, and the real implication of all this is not what Descartes and Locke took it to be. Colours etc. are not unknown arrangements of primary qualities. Colour, heat and other 'secondary qualities' are in fact features of mental substance that are erroneously projected onto material objects. Pierre Bayle, another notable French philosopher influenced by Malebranche and with whose work Berkeley was very familiar, held this view of secondary qualities as well. According to the 'new philosophy ... Heat, smells, colours and the like are not in the objects of the senses. They are modifications of the senses. I know that bodies are not at all as they appear to me.'[46] Malebranche and Bayle take the new philosophy to have unsettling consequences for our ordinary view of what qualities objects possess, on the ground that the claim that colours are non-resembling causes of ideas; a very distant idea from our ordinary conception of colours and other such qualities.

Berkeley agrees with Malebranche and Bayle on this implication of the mechanical philosophy.[47] He thinks that any version of the primary/secondary quality distinction profoundly disturbs our natural view of what qualities physical objects possess and our knowledge of them. It has the implication that what we take the world to be is either an illusion born of ignorance (in the case of Locke) or the projection of sensory ideas onto the world (in the case of Malebranche). In either case, the world as we experience it is a 'false imaginary glare' (DHP2

---

[45] *Search*, p. 441.
[46] Note *b* to Pyrrho, in Pierre Bayle, *Historical and Critical Dictionary, Selections*, trans. R. Popkin (Indianapolis, IN: Hackett, 1991), p. 197.
[47] See Chapter 5, section 3.

211). Berkeley seeks to restore to real things the properties they appear to have. 'I differ from the Cartesians in that I make extension, and Colour etc. to exist really in Bodies & independent of Our Mind.[48] All y^s carefully & lucidly to be set forth' (PC 801).

6 CAUSATION AND POWERS

Berkeley sees in the philosophy of materialism endemic threats of sceptical ignorance (we do not know the essence of material things), Cartesian scepticism (we cannot know that there are material objects that cause our ideas), and the idea that our ordinary conception of the world is nothing but a 'false imaginary glare'. He also believes that, properly thought through, matter does not really explain anything at all, either because the nature of this explanation is too obscure to be explanatory or because matter is simply redundant.

At the risk of oversimplification, the general thought behind materialism is that the behaviour of all physical objects could be understood in terms of matter in states of motion and rest. Changes in these states involve the impact of material objects on one another. How such a vision is to be spelled out in detail is difficult enough, but this difficulty is compounded by some fundamental metaphysical problems. Most notable is the ordinary belief (imprecise as it may be) that physical objects have the power to affect other things. Locke distinguishes, as others did, between *active* and *passive* powers, between that which is able to *make* change and that able to *receive* it.[49] However, our understanding of these powers is very limited. Fires burn, and the sun melts wax, and for Locke we can go some way to understanding phenomena such as these in terms of microscopic particles interacting with each other. All these transactions involve the 'communication of motion by impulse'.[50] But just *how* is that possible and in just *what* does it consist? By what power? The 'active power of Moving', as Locke puts it, 'hardly comes within our comprehension'.[51] The same is true with regard to our own activity: that our thought causes matter to move is something we have daily experience of, but *how* is not something that we understand. Again, Locke is sceptical about our

---

[48] But not independent of *all* minds, see Chapter 6, section 3, pp. 93–98.   [49] E 2.21.2.
[50] E 2.23.28.   [51] E 2.23.28.

capacity to understand the world. Material objects have (probably) a mixture of active and passive powers, but these we cannot understand. Our idea of active power is an imperfect one, drawn from reflecting on our wills. This Lockean modesty both influences and is influenced by Newton's own, who in his philosophy took matter and motion to be insufficient to explain all natural phenomena. Most notably, but not exclusively, among these phenomena is gravitational influence which appeared to require bodies to influence each other at a distance.[52] Science is ultimately a matter of deriving fundamental regularities or laws of nature without pretending to understand what grounds these laws.

Berkeley is unsatisfied with Locke's modesty, taking it to be ultimately an admission that we cannot explain anything by appeal to material substance.[53] He has more sympathy with Malebranche, who denied that material objects are endowed with powers. For Malebranche there is only one true cause (that is, anything with genuine power) and that is God. Material objects are not 'second causes' (that is, objects with powers, which, though ultimately derived from God, are nevertheless efficacious). The collusion of bodies is the 'occasion' for God to act and bring about change. Occasionalism is perhaps Malebranche's most famous doctrine, though not one original to him, and although it might look strange, it is supported by a battery of very powerful arguments. Berkeley subsequently exploits an obvious weak point in this theory. If matter is causally inert, and all power resides in God, then, to put it bluntly, what is the use of matter? 'The Sillyness of the Current Doctrine', noted Berkeley, 'makes much for me. They commonly suppose a material world . . . [which] according to their own confession to no purpose, all our sensations may be & sometimes actually are without them' (PC 476).

Berkeley's rejection of Lockean modesty and occasionalist matter opens up a new way to understand the world. Real things are a special class of the immediate objects of sense. They are not material substances that exist without our mind. They are not objects whose essences and causal powers we do not understand, or utterly

---

[52] For a useful discussion of this predicament, see Stephen Buckle, 'British Sceptical Realism: A Fresh Look at the British Tradition', *European Journal of Philosophy* 7 (1999), 1–29.
[53] See Chapter 5, section 4, pp. 77–79 and Chapter 7, section 3, p. 126.

redundant external things. They are coloured in just the way they seem to be, and taste the way they seem. But what then is the role of science? If science is the investigation into the deeper causal structure of the world, Berkeley's conception of the world appears to deprive science of its very object. Berkeley, who is as aware as anyone of the evident progress of the sciences of his day, has a radical view of the aims and practices of science. Science seeks to understand the world, and Berkeley's world is a world of ideas. Science seeks to understand the relations between worldly objects – ideas – but the relevant relation is not that of cause and effect, but *sign* and *signified*. The sequence of ideas constituting the world is a *language* by which God communicates with human beings, and understanding the world is the interpretation of that language. We glimpse, in normal life, some sentences from the book of nature, but science aims to decipher or interpret much more of it.[54]

7 ATHEISM AND IRRELIGION

Malebranche hoped that his philosophy embodied the Pauline doctrine, expressed in Acts 17:28, that it is God 'in whom we live, and move and have our being'.[55] Our dependence on God's ideas to perceive the world and the location of true power in God is one way in which this doctrine is given philosophical articulation. Berkeley's philosophy has this aim too, and he quotes the Pauline dictum at PHK §149. Both philosophers think that their philosophies bring us close to God, or at least closer than other philosophies. But why does material substance lead to irreligion?

One source of irreligion Malebranche identifies relates to the doctrine of second causes. Roughly put, power is worthy of worship, and if objects have their own active powers, as Locke maintained, they become objects of idolatry. For this reason Malebranche claims that the doctrine of 'secondary causes' is 'the most dangerous error' of ancient philosophy.[56] Berkeley agrees that secondary causes encourage idolatry, and a pleasing consequence of his philosophy is that that the only genuine power at work in the world is the will of God, thus undermining idolatry (PHK §94). But Berkeley saw deeper threats at

---

[54] See further, Chapter 7, sections 1, 2 and 3.   [55] *Search*, p. 235.   [56] *Search*, p. 446.

work in the doctrine of material substance. Nowadays we think of 'atheism' as simply a denial of the existence of God, but matters were rather less clear-cut during the early modern period, and the term 'atheism' was a flexible form of derogatory address. So all sorts of views are what Berkeley calls 'atheism a little disguised'.[57] One is 'materialism', understood as the claim that everything, including thinking things, is material. Locke's general modesty about our knowledge of material substance led him to speculate briefly whether material substance, rather than an immaterial soul, might have the power to think. God could 'if he please, superadd to Matter a Faculty of thinking'.[58] Locke's intention in this speculation was to illustrate our ignorance, but he kick-started the belief that the mind is material, and because material, naturally mortal. Berkeley is well aware of this, writing in his notebook 'candidly to take Notice that Locke holds some dangerous opinions, such as ... The Possibility of Matter's Thinking' (PC 695),[59] and to show that its implication for the natural mortality of the soul is 'atheism little disguised'. Another form of 'atheism little disguised' is the metaphysical system of Benedict Spinoza, who was widely held to argue that God was identical to self-caused extended matter, and widely perceived to be an atheist.[60] Again, if the world is material, is not human action determined by the laws that govern the material world? Spinoza and Thomas Hobbes thought so, and their claims that such a position was compatible with human freedom were widely held to be either insincere or, at best, insufficient. So atheists 'little disguised' include those who 'deny the freedom ... of the soul' and also deny 'all moral effects and natural religion, [and] deny Him to be an observer, judge and rewarder of actions', and are atheists 'little disguised'. The possible self-subsistence of material substance is itself a possible encouragement to atheism. If matter does have powers, why not think that it is self-caused? On the Lockean picture the world seems to operate through its own powers, making it seemingly independent of God, and God himself an absentee landlord.

[57] *Theory of Vision Vindicated and Explained* (§6).   [58] E 4.3.6.
[59] This threat is removed when matter is removed, something Berkeley notes at PHK §93.
[60] Berkeley writes that on his system the 'Philosophers lose their matter ... the Profane their Extended Deity' (PC 391). (Cf. PC 825, where Locke is named.)

8 BERKELEY'S RESPONSE AND COMMON SENSE

Having sketched the broad contours of the philosophical milieu against which Berkeley was reacting, let us now sketch his reaction, bringing together the points made earlier. Berkeley rejects material substance entirely and holds that physical reality is composed of what we immediately perceive. Our perceptual relation to the world is direct. There is no sceptical gap between ideas that represent 'external objects' and the objects themselves. There is no mysterious hidden essence to the world that eludes us because our limited faculties are such as to preclude our grasp of the nature of the material world that underpins the world we experience. The world is composed solely of what we immediately perceive, and so there is nothing in principle that eludes our sense experience. Nor is there an invidious distinction between how the world 'really' is and how it shows up to us in ordinary experience. Objects really are coloured (*pace* Malebranche) and colours, tastes, etc. are just how we take them to be and not some mysterious material powers (*pace* Locke). There is no mysterious or unintelligible relation between mind and matter. We are brought closer to God in the world since it operates by his direct and intimate action.

Berkeley accuses materialism of 'scepticism and paradox', and claims that it is his philosophy, not materialism, which is faithful to common sense. He claims that he 'side[s] in all things with the Mob' (PC 405), and that the 'vulgar' or pre-philosophical understanding of the existence of unperceived objects agrees with his view (PC 408). But central to immaterialism is the claim that real things, which are those immediately perceived by sense, have no existence without the mind. Is this not the real affront to common sense? And was W. B. Yeats not right when he later claimed that 'God-appointed Berkeley ... proved all things a dream'? The topic of Berkeley's immaterialism's relation to common sense is a complex one at the level of detail, and we shall touch upon some of these during the course of this book, but two general remarks are worth making. First, Berkeley denies that objects exist independently of perception. This is supposedly anti-common sense on the grounds that we do believe that tables or chairs exist independently of being perceived. Berkeley, however, presents an interesting case that we do *not* really believe that they so exist. The very supposition of perception-independent existence is incoherent and it is impossible really to believe something that it is incoherent.[61] So his view is not at odds with common sense, but only with a mistaken philosophy. Secondly, it is an open question whether his opposition – the doctrine of material substance – is in line with common sense. The doctrine retains the (supposedly) common-sense view that material objects exist independently of our perception of them, but at a price. It introduces the prospect of Cartesian scepticism by making the immediate objects of awareness not the objects themselves, but ideas or representations. Even without the threat of scepticism, this view of our perceptual engagement is something Berkeley takes to be at odds with common sense. We think that we perceive real things rather than representations of real things. Furthermore, the way the world appears to be in sense experience is radically different from how it is itself. Our perceptual-based picture of the world is nothing but a 'false imaginary glare' compared with the scientific conception of the world. Berkeley seeks to restore the world as directly perceived and just as how it seems to be, and so in that sense brings us back to common sense.

[61] See Chapter 5, section 5, pp. 79–82.

CHAPTER 3

The Introduction to the Principles

I INTRODUCTION TO THE INTRODUCTION

The Introduction to the *Principles* can be divided into roughly three parts. The first part, §§1–6, suggests that scepticism is not due to a defect in, or the limitations of, human faculties, but is an illusion fostered by the mistakes of philosophers and, in particular, mistakes about language. Implicit here is Berkeley's view that the whole edifice of the mechanical philosophy discussed in the previous chapter, which is itself the source of scepticism, is a delusion born of misunderstanding ordinary language. One particular mistake is singled out by Berkeley, namely, the philosophical 'opinion that the mind hath a power of framing *abstract ideas*' (PHK I §6). The second part of the Introduction (§§7–18) consists of his celebrated critique of these abstract ideas. The remainder identifies the cause of the mistaken belief in abstract ideas as language, discusses some different functions of language, and warns against the general danger attendant to the 'embarras and delusion of words' (PHK I §25).

Berkeley worked very hard on the Introduction. We have a draft version that is much longer than the published version, and both it and the published version are philosophically rich and interesting. But the Introduction is also deeply puzzling. Abstraction, materialism and the scepticism generated by materialism are somehow connected. Thus, in the main body of *Principles* Berkeley tells us that the 'opinion strangely prevailing amongst men, that . . . sensible objects have existence . . . distinct from their being perceived' (PHK §4) 'depend[s] on the doctrine of *abstract ideas*' (PHK §5). But just what these connections are is, to say the very least, extremely opaque.[1] Indeed, the relation between the Introduction and the main body of the *Principles* is quite generally puzzling: as Jonathan Dancy writes 'Perhaps the greatest mystery of the *Principles* is the relation between the Introduction and the main text.'[2] In this chapter we shall confine ourselves to understanding the Introduction itself. First, we discuss Berkeley's view of the sources of scepticism. Then, we examine his critique of 'abstract ideas', before turning to his general remarks on language. Later on in this book we shall connect these various themes with the main body of the *Principles* and try to dispel some of the mystery.

2 LEARNED DUST

The opening sections of the Introduction contrast the attitudes of common sense with the views of philosophy, and reveal Berkeley's distinctive attitude to scepticism. Most of mankind 'walk the high-road of plain, common sense', where nothing familiar 'appears unaccountable or difficult to comprehend', and human beings are 'out of all danger of becoming *sceptics*' (PHK I §1). Philosophers who follow reason are, on the other hand, led away from this road, and become embroiled in difficulties that threaten to leave them sat 'down in a forlorn scepticism' (PHK I §1). What accounts for such a forlorn scepticism?

A 'forlorn scepticism' might emerge because philosophical reflection shows that the beliefs comprising common sense are inherently problematic. Our belief that there are physical objects or other persons might turn out to lack support or even be incapable of being justified. We might think that we have evidence for such things, but find, on reflection, that we have, or can have, no such evidence. Some of the central beliefs upon which others rest might be false, or have unacceptable implications. We might think that we are directly aware of physical objects, but philosophy 'discovers' we are only directly aware of ideas. We might think that we can only know something if

---

[1] 'If you cannot see [the link between the two], that is because it is so tenuous as to be almost invisible.' Jonathan Bennett, *Learning from Six Philosophers: Descartes, Spinoza, Leibniz, Locke, Berkeley, Hume*, 2 vols. (Oxford University Press, 2001), vol. 2, p. 146.

[2] George Berkeley, 'Editor's introduction', *A Treatise Concerning the Principles of Human Knowledge*, ed. J. Dancy (Oxford University Press, 1998), p. 28.

we know that we know it. But if we do hold that view, it becomes impossible to have knowledge. Common sense, though perhaps adequate for everyday life, is pregnant with scepticism, and philosophical reflection acts as midwife to it. The difference between the philosophers and the non-philosophers is that the former reflects on common sense and becomes aware of its sceptical implications and the latter lives a life of blissful ignorance.

This is not Berkeley's view. For him the doubts of the forlorn sceptic are unreal or 'unnatural'.[3] The beliefs that comprise common sense do not have sceptical implications. Instead, the doubts come from a mistaken philosophical *account* of common sense. In other words, Berkeley rejects the idea that scepticism is generated by 'the obscurity of things, or the natural weakness and imperfection of our understandings' (PHK I §2). For him 'the far greater part, if not all, of those difficulties that have hitherto amused philosophers, and blocked up the way to knowledge, are entirely owing to ourselves. That we have first raised a dust, and then complain, we cannot see' (PHK I §3). We saw in the previous chapter that materialism generated a Cartesian scepticism about the existence of the external world and a Lockean scepticism about our capacity to understand that world. To remove the unnatural doubts we need to identify the philosophical principles that engender confusion, and Berkeley promises to 'discover what those principles are, which have introduced all that doubtfulness and uncertainty, those absurdities and contradictions into the several sects of philosophy' (PHK I §4).

The fundamental source of such unnatural doubts is the misunderstanding of language. One error that misunderstanding language generates is that 'the mind hath a power of framing *abstract ideas* or notions of things', which in turn is a source of 'innumerable errors and difficulties in almost all parts of knowledge' (PHK I §6). The mistake that we have such a power is the source of materialism which engenders the unnatural sceptical doubts. It is for this reason that the centrepiece of Berkeley's Introduction is an assault on abstract ideas. We will not be able to understand the connection between abstraction

---

[3] For a view that has some affinities with Berkeley's attitude to scepticism, see Michael Williams, *Unnatural Doubts: Epistemological Realism and the Basis of Scepticism* (Princeton University Press, 1995).

and materialism until we understand what abstraction is supposed to be and why Berkeley rejects it, and it is to this that we now turn.

3 AGAINST ABSTRACT IDEAS: TWO READINGS

What are 'abstract ideas'? Abstract ideas relate to our capacity to think and to talk about things in general rather than particular things. We can think and talk about redness as opposed to that particular shade of red, and think and talk of people in general rather than particular persons like Teddy or Edmund. One account of our capacity to do this invokes the non-sensory intellect and its grasp of quasi-platonic inherently general ideas that reside in the mind of God. But Berkeley agrees with Locke in rejecting the intellect and holding that there exist no 'universals' or inherently general entities that exist over and above particular things. There is this or that instance of redness, but no redness itself. So how then is general thought and talk possible? According to Locke, or at least how Berkeley understands him, the mind creates new ideas that represent general things, arrived at through a *process* of abstraction from our experience of particular things. These supposedly explain our capacity to think and reason about the general, and provide meanings for general terms. It is these that are abstract ideas, and it is these that Berkeley thinks are impossible.

Berkeley considers three different kinds of abstract idea, the first of which is discussed at PHK I §7. We can think of the particular qualities any given object has and consider how two or more objects might resemble each other in these respects. For example, there are two copies of a book on my desk, the covers of which are both a particular shade of green. Now, the particular greenness of the book on my left is not something that exists independently of the book's particular shape. Nevertheless, I can think of that quality independently of the book and compare it to the quality of the other. I can do this because I can form the idea or concept of that shade of green independently of the particular shape of the book by abstraction. I can form the concept of that shade of green, even though that shade does not exist independently of the other qualities that constitute the particular object. So while it is not 'possible for colour . . . to exist without extension . . . the mind can frame to itself by *abstraction* the idea of colour exclusive of extension' (PHK I §7).

The first kind of abstract idea, then, explains our capacity to think of qualities. The second kind of abstraction is introduced at PHK I §8, and concerns what philosophers discuss in terms of a distinction between *determinables* and *determinates*. Everything that is coloured is some particular colour or other, and everything that has shape has some particular shape or other. Shape is a determinable of an object, and being triangular is a determinate of shape. Colour is a determinable of an object, and redness is a particular determinate of colour. While everything that exists is a determinate we can nevertheless think of the determinables. We can think of colour in general as well as particular colours, and we can think of shape in general as well as particular shapes. By noticing what, for example, distinguishes coloured things, the mind 'makes an idea of colour in abstract which is neither red, nor blue, nor white, nor any other determinate colour' (PHK I §8).

So we supposedly have abstract ideas of determinate qualities and abstract ideas of determinables. PHK I §9 considers a further category of abstract ideas that concern not qualities but *kinds*. A human being is a 'compounded object', a compound of particular determinate qualities. Any particular human has a determinate hair colour, eye colour, height and so on, and every human differs from another in one or more of these qualities, and to a greater or lesser extent. How do we then think about human beings in general, rather than only this or that human? The answer is that we form an idea by abstracting from, or leaving out, all that is peculiar to the particular persons. The

mind having observed that Peter, James, and John, resemble each other, in certain common agreements of shape and other qualities, leaves out of the complex or compounded idea it has of Peter, James, and any other particular man, that which is peculiar to each, retaining only what is common to all (PHK I §9)

Why does Berkeley think there are no abstract ideas of any of these kinds? He makes a somewhat tart personal report that he lacks this 'wonderful faculty' of forming abstract ideas (PHK I §10), later observing that it is implausible that before children 'prate together, of their sugar-plums and rattles and the rest of their little trinkets' they have to make the great effort required to form abstract ideas (PHK I §14). The tone of these remarks suggests that Berkeley is forgetting his memo to himself to 'rein in y^r Satyrical nature' (PC 634), and, indeed, these complaints do not constitute his real objection to abstract ideas. His real objection is not that such ideas are difficult to form. His real objection is that such ideas are impossible. There are two broad interpretations of why he thinks they are impossible. One way to read Berkeley is to take him to suppose that all ideas are must be mental images, and the images required for the alleged abstract ideas are impossible.[4] Call this the argument from imagism. The second way sees Berkeley holding that we cannot conceive an impossibility, and that what abstract ideas purport to represent are themselves impossibilities. To conceive of anything is to form an idea of it. But the objects supposedly represented in abstract ideas are impossibilities, so there can be no such ideas.[5] Call this the argument from impossibility. Each reading has its own advantages and its own disadvantages. We need to decide between these two readings because which reading we take will affect how we understand the vexed issues of the connection between abstraction and immaterialism. In this section I shall introduce the two readings and suggest that Berkeley's real argument is the argument from impossibility.

Let us begin with the argument from imagism. We noted in Chapter 2, section 2 that Locke took ideas to be images that represent primarily by resemblance. An image is about a swan when the image resembles a swan, and image is about a clock when it resembles a clock. Berkeley also thinks that ideas can resemble other ideas. Ideas are the resembling copies or *images* of perceptual experiences and constitute the contents of the *imagination*.[6] The mind possesses '*ideas*, or *images* of things, which they [the things ideas represent] copy and represent' (PHK §33). So, on the argument from imagism, Berkeley's objections derive from the alleged fact that there could be no images of the sort required for any of the three forms of abstract ideas described above.

---

[4] For this reading, see, for example, George Pitcher, *Berkeley* (London: Routledge, 1977), ch. 5, and more recently, Bennett, *Learning from Six Philosophers*, vol. 2, pp. 17–21.

[5] For this reading, see, for example, Kenneth Winkler, *Berkeley: An Interpretation* (Oxford: Clarendon Press, 1989), ch. 2; Douglas Jesseph, *Berkeley's Philosophy of Mathematics* (University of Chicago Press, 1993), pp. 20–7; and, more recently, John Russell Roberts, *A Metaphysics for the Mob: The Philosophy of George Berkeley* (New York: Oxford University Press, 2007), pp. 46–9.

[6] These, too, are ideas, but we shall reserve discussion of this until the next chapter.

Why? The first kind of abstract idea is an idea of a particular quality abstracted from some other quality from which it is otherwise inseparable. I can think about the colour of an object even if that colour must have some kind of shape. The objection to such an account of abstract ideas is that one cannot imagine – form an image of – a colour without its having some kind of shape. So the abstract idea of a particular quality independent of shape seems an impossible image to form. Consider now the idea of some determinable like colour. What kind of image could serve as an idea of the determinable 'colour', an image that is no particular colour or, as Berkeley puts it, an 'idea . . . which is neither red, nor blue, nor white, nor any other determinate colour' (PHK I §8)? Finally, what kind of image could serve as the abstract idea of kinds of compound beings? Consider PHK I §13 where Berkeley seizes upon some remarks Locke makes about the abstract idea of a triangle. Any triangle is either scalene, isosceles or equilateral ('equicural'). Can we have an image of a triangle that is *none* of these? Or, if the idea of triangle is supposed somehow to represent the fact that triangles are either scalene, isosceles or equilateral, must the image somehow be scalene *and* isosceles *and* equilateral? Or is the idea supposed to be 'all and none of these at once' (PHK I 13)?[7]

Reading Berkeley in this manner leaves him vulnerable to a number of objections. Perhaps the most telling is that his objection rests on a mistaken view of mental imagery. Berkeley must assume that mental images are both *determinate* and *saturated* with detail. He assumes that when I imagine a cat, say, I must imagine it to have a particular number of stripes, each of a particular shade, his tail in a particular position, his eyes open or shut, etc. It must be determinate with respect to all its determinables and must be fully detailed. However, mental images are not like that. If I ask you to imagine a stripy cat, there may be no fact of the matter regarding the number of stripes it has (it can be indeterminate in that respect). Return now to the images supposedly involved in the third kind of abstraction. Considered this way, in forming an image of cat I need not have an image of something that has a particular fur colour. Nor need it be saturated in detail

---

[7] In the *Commentaries* Berkeley speaks of this 'killing blow' against abstract ideas in connection with Locke's triangle example (PC 687).

(the complex sheen that the light on casts on different parts of his body need be no part of an image). The image might simply be cat-shaped and not involve all the detail that, say, a photograph of a cat has. Given this, the image that serves as an abstract idea of a cat might be something like a vague stick figure.

It should, however, be noted that this objection to the argument from imaginism has its limits, for there are limits to the extent to which an image can be indeterminate or lacking in detail.[8] I might be able to form an image of a cat with an indeterminate number of stripes, but can I form an image of a triangle that is really indeterminate between scalene, isosceles or equilateral? With respect to the second kind of abstraction, it seems near impossible to have an image of a colour that is somehow indeterminate with respect to its colour, and perhaps the same is so of a shapeless image of colour. Whatever the case may be, however, I think the argument from impossibility is a more promising interpretation of what animates Berkeley against abstract ideas. For one thing, while Berkeley never draws any explicit link between images and his critique of abstract ideas, there is some textual evidence for his using the argument from impossibility. Berkeley holds that if some putative objects or states of affairs are themselves impossible, we cannot think or form ideas of impossibilities. But the things represented by alleged abstract ideas are themselves impossibilities. So we cannot form ideas of them.

Read this way his arguments rest on the general thesis that we cannot conceive (form an idea of) any impossible object. His explicit commitment to this thesis occurs not in the published but in the draft Introduction. Berkeley writes:

It is, I think, a receiv'd axiom than an impossibility cannot be conceiv'd. For what created intelligence will pretend to conceive, that which God cannot cause to be? Now it is on all hands agreed, that nothing abstract or general can be made really to exist, whence it should seem to follow, that it cannot have so much as an ideal existence in the understanding.[9]

His argument in the published version can be seen to rest on the 'received axiom' even though this is not explicitly stated in the published Introduction. Consider again the first kind of abstract

---

[8] As was said by Pitcher, *Berkeley*, pp. 70–1.
[9] In Luce and Jessop (eds.), *The Works of George Berkeley*, vol. 2, p. 125.

idea, the idea of a particular quality separated from those other qualities that it is impossible to separate (a colour without a shape, for example). But if it really is impossible, we cannot conceive it. So, Berkeley writes:

> I own myself able to abstract in one sense, as when I consider some particular parts or qualities separated from others, with which though they are united in some object, yet, it is possible they may really exist without them. But I deny that I can abstract from one another, or conceive separately, those qualities *which it is impossible should exist so separated*; or that I can frame a general notion by abstracting from particulars in the manner aforesaid. (PHK I §10, added emphasis)

These last two forms of abstraction he calls 'the proper acceptations of *abstraction*'. Notice the contrast between the first sense of abstraction, which Berkeley allows, and the second, which he rejects, turns on what is possible and impossible. That clearly fits the argument from impossibility. And it easy to see how it fits the other two cases too. In the case of the second kind of abstract idea we are supposed to be able to form an idea of colour in general as opposed to ideas of this or that particular colour. But it is impossible that there can be a colour that is no particular colour. If it is impossible, then we cannot form an idea of it. We can say the *words* 'a colour that is no particular colour' all right, but that does not show that those words express an idea. Finally, turning to the example of the triangle, the concept 'triangle' implies that it must be scalene, isosceles or equilateral, and there cannot be triangles that are *none* of these or *all* of these at once. Nor could there be a person who has all hair colours at once or none at all.

The argument from impossibility is explicitly stated in *Alciphron*, where we get this exchange:

EUPHRANOR: Pray, Alciphron, which are those things you would call absolutely impossible?
ALCIPHRON: Such as include a contradiction.
EUPHRANOR: Can you frame an idea of what includes a contradiction?
ALCIPHRON: I cannot.
EUPHRANOR: Consequently, whatever is absolutely impossible you cannot form an idea of?
ALCIPHRON: This I grant.
EUPHRANOR: But can a colour or triangle, such as you describe their abstract general ideas, really exist?

ALCIPHRON: It is absolutely impossible such things should exist in Nature.
EUPHRANOR: Should it not follow, then, that they cannot exist in your
      mind, or, in other words, that you cannot conceive or frame an idea of
      them?[10]

Here we get the argument from impossibility, and an account of that
in which impossibility consists, namely, where a contradiction is
implied in the description of the object. Admittedly, there is no
explicit mention of the thesis that an impossibility is inconceivable
in the published version of the Introduction, and the exchange quoted
above was dropped in later editions of the *Alciphron*. Nevertheless, the
cumulative effect strongly suggests that the argument from impossibility is Berkeley's strategy.

     Still, some commentators object that this cannot be Berkeley's real
objection. The argument from impossibility cannot be Berkeley's
argument, they suggest, because it rests on a serious mistake about
representation.[11] If Berkeley thinks that abstract ideas must be representations of impossibilities, he must think that a general or abstract
representation of, say, a triangle is either a representation of a triangle
lacking properties it must have (being neither scalene nor isosceles, etc.)
or a representation of a triangle *having incompatible properties* (being
both scalene and isosceles). However, representations can be *silent* on
features of the objects they represent. To understand what is meant by
'silence' consider the following example. Suppose I show you a
photograph of the Hancock Tower in Chicago. The picture does
not show any persons inside the building (you can see no one looking
out of the window). Does it follow from that that the picture is a
representation *of the tower containing no people*? Not at all – it is simply
a representation of the tower that is completely *silent* on whether or
not someone is inside. To put it another way, the absence of people
in the photograph is not a *representation of the absence of people*. It is
silent on whether or how many people are in it. It is simply a
representation of the tower. So we could have a general or abstract
representation of a triangle that is neither a representation of a triangle
that is neither scalene nor isosceles, etc., or of a triangle *that is both scalene*

---

[10] *Works*, vol. 2, pp. 333–4.
[11] See Pitcher, *Berkeley*, pp. 67–70, and, more recently, Bennett, *Learning from Six Philosophers*,
      vol. 2, pp. 17–19.

and isosceles etc. It is simply a representation of a triangle, a representation that is silent on the matter of what kind of triangle the triangle is. We can therefore attribute the argument from impossibility to Berkeley, but only on the assumption that he is making a silly mistake, so it is better not to attribute it to him at all.

However, I think Berkeley makes an assumption about how abstract ideas are supposed to represent that implies that they cannot be silent in the required way, and this explains why he rejects abstract ideas on the basis of the argument from impossibility. This assumption emerges from the way he reads Locke. To understand the assumption and how it explains Berkeley's use of the argument from impossibility let us now turn to how Berkeley understood Locke.

4 BERKELEY'S READING OF LOCKE ON ABSTRACT IDEAS

Locke is evidently Berkeley's primary target in the Introduction. But commentators frequently complain that Berkeley's understanding of Locke's account of abstract ideas is at best unsympathetic and at worst completely mistaken. Now, I agree it might be true that Berkeley ultimately misreads Locke, but in Berkeley's defence it is actually a rather difficult and contested matter to say quite what Locke's own views really are, and even if Berkeley does get Locke wrong, this mistake is forgivable. Locke sends mixed messages, as it were, regarding what he really means.[12] Rather than try to decide what Locke's views really are, it is more useful to consider how those mixed messages might have encouraged Berkeley's own understanding of what an abstract is supposed to be.

Locke writes:

the Mind makes the particular *Ideas*, received from particular Objects, to become general; which is done by *considering* them as they are in the Mind such Appearances, separate from all other Existences ... This is called ABSTRACTION, whereby *Ideas* taken from particular Beings, become general Representatives of all the same kind.[13]

---

[12] For two very different views on what abstract ideas are for Locke, see Ayers, *Locke*, vol. 1, pp. 250–1 and Bennett, *Learning from Six Philosophers*, vol. 2, pp. 16–17.
[13] E 2.11.9, my emphasis on 'considering'.

Notice that Locke talks of *considering* particular ideas 'separate from all other existences', rather than separating ideas from other ideas. It is not the case that when we form an abstract idea of some quality that some *new* idea is formed by separation or abstraction from particulars. We engage in an activity of *considering* them separately or partially, and then use these selectively considered particular ideas to stand for that general kind. Again, '*Ideas* become general, by separating from them the circumstances of Time and Place, and any other *Ideas*, that may determine them to this or that particular Existence. By this way of abstraction, they are made capable of representing more Individuals than one.'[14] We *use* a particular idea through selective attention as a representation of other qualities of the same kind. Similarly, when Locke describes the abstract ideas of kinds there is much to suggest selective attention is at play. Having observed several individual humans in the world, their differences and their similarities, they 'frame an *Idea*, which they find those many Particulars do partake in; and to that they give, with others, the name *Man*', and in doing so we 'make nothing new, but only leave out of the complex idea they had of *Peter* and *James*, *Mary* and *Jane*, that which is peculiar to each'.[15] This leaving out is not a matter of omitting detail by *removing* things from the mental image, but simply of ignoring what is particular to it and selectively attending only to commonalities.

If abstraction for Locke is merely selective attention, then Berkeley's objections are misplaced on either the argument from imagism or the argument from impossibility readings. Locke is not inviting us to form the impossible image of a colour without extension. Our abstract idea of red is simply a particular idea of red that we separately attend to, ignoring its shape or extension. If Berkeley's objection is that we are attempting to represent an impossibility, it would again fail. In attending to the colour separately we are not attempting to conceive it *existing* separately from shape – something that is impossible for it to do. We are representing solely the colour, a representation that is silent with respect to shape. This is unfortunate, not least because Berkeley appears to think, just like Locke, that we can separately attend to particular ideas.

---

[14] E 3.3.6.   [15] E 3.3.7.

However, some of what Locke writes suggests something different. It suggests that abstraction is the formation of a new distinct idea, rather than a matter of selectively attending to some particular one. Locke tells us that we create a *new* idea, made 'not by an additions' but by 'leaving out' properties like shape,[16] and a little later he says that we make 'a new distinct complex idea'.[17] This can suggest that general thought is made possible by the creation of new ideas that are inherently general in their character rather than our selectively attending to particular ideas. So Berkeley may have fastened on phrases like these and assumed that we come to represent generality not by selective attention, but through the formation of new distinct ideas that by *themselves* represent generality. He thinks of them as '*abstract, determinate ideas*, which constitute the true and only immediate signification of each general name' (PHK I §18).

If Berkeley does understand abstract ideas to be distinct ideas created by abstraction from original ones, what bearing does this have on the objection to the argument from impossibility considered in the previous section? The first thing to note is that ideas are partly introduced by Locke because he thought them necessary for thinking or representation. Thoughts or representations are *about* other things. Philosophers use the term 'intentional object' to specify what one's thought is about. Intentional objects need not be real objects in the ordinary sense of the word 'real'. My thought about a unicorn has a unicorn as its intentional object, but unicorns do not exist. But in order to explain how one thought is about one thing and another thought about another Locke invokes mental objects – ideas or images – which assist in individuating one thought from another. However, while images are *necessary* for thinking, a particular image does not uniquely determine the intentional object of your thought (that is, what it is your thought is *about*). This is where selective attention comes into play. An image of a red patch before my mind is necessary in order for me to think about redness, but precisely what I am thinking – the 'content' of my thought – is not fully determined by that idea before my mind. Through selectively attending to the idea my thought is about the redness rather than the red patch, and I could use the

---

[16] E 3.3.8.   [17] E 3.3.9.

same idea to think about shape. Although those objects are images, what we can think about is not solely down to those images themselves, but the images *plus* the ways in which we can attend to them. So there are two different thoughts about different things, but both using the same idea. My capacity to represent redness in a way that is silent about shape is not down to the object or idea alone, but the object and my mental selection.

What though, as Berkeley might assume, if abstract ideas are new objects that *by themselves* determine uniquely and exhaustively the intentional object of thought? It must itself be a new object in virtue of which it represents its intentional object, but its being a new object makes it impossible for it to be silent in the way required. What your thought is about must be determined by the object itself, and objects themselves cannot be silent. For the object to represent triangularity and yet be silent, the object itself must be an object that is neither scalene, equilateral nor isosceles or none of these.[18] There is no way for any such object to be silent on this score, and so it would have to be a representation of an impossibility. It would also itself have to *be* an impossible object. Now this is not to deny that Berkeley assumed that such mental objects are, or must be, mental images. But the objection to abstract ideas is subtly different from the argument from images. The argument from impossibility, when combined with the claim that the intentional object of a thought must be determined solely and exhaustively by an object 'before the mind', leaves it impossible for there to be silent representations. Any idea of a triangle must involve an image, and if that image is supposed to determine exactly and exhaustively just what your thought is about it cannot be silent on being scalene or anything else.

If this is right, we can see why Berkeley thinks that argument from impossibility succeeds. This does not excuse his misreading of Locke, of course, but it does help us to understand the nature of his objection. Abstract ideas are impossible because no impossibility can be conceived. Knowing this, as we shall see, helps us to understand the connection between abstraction and immaterialism.

---

[18] For similar, but by no means identical, considerations regarding Berkeley and abstraction, see Winkler, *Berkeley: An Interpretation*, ch. 2.

5 LANGUAGE, CONFUSION AND FUNCTION

Berkeley not only criticises the doctrine of abstract ideas, but also diagnoses the philosophical illness of which it is a symptom. The belief that we have abstract ideas is born of a mistake about language, and in particular the mistake that 'every significant name stands for an idea' (PHK I §19). As we mentioned briefly in the last chapter, this is Locke's view.[19] It is evident, Berkeley tells us, that we use general terms or 'universal signs' like 'triangle' or 'red', but on the assumption that these must stand for individual ideas philosophers assume that there are *'abstract, determinate ideas*, which constitute the true and only immediate signification of each general name' (PHK I §18). Berkeley rightly points out that words can be used to do things other than stand as signs for ideas (see below). Locke's mistake that every meaningful term must mark an idea leads him to think that there are abstract ideas, as follows. Since 'names, which yet are not thought altogether insignificant, do not always mark out particular conceivable ideas, it is straightaway concluded that they stand for abstract notions' (PHK I §19).

Berkeley does not deny that we can use general language. General speech and thought are possible because a particular idea (a particular triangle, say) can become general 'by being made to represent or stand for all other particular ideas of the same sort' (PHK I §12). This suggests that our generalising is accounted for by our conventional *uses* of a sign, rather than owing itself to the presence of a special class of inherently general representations. As it is our use of such signs that allows us to converse without the need of abstract ideas, and we can use particular ideas as conventional signs, Berkeley thinks abstract ideas are not 'a whit more needful for the *enlargement of knowledge* than for *communication*' (PHK I §15). Here he picks out what he takes to be Locke's view of the role of abstract ideas of mathematical demonstration. Locke, according to Berkeley, claims that abstract ideas are required to determine what is universal of triangularity. To know, for example, that it is true of every triangle that its angles sum to 180° its truth must be demonstrated on the abstract or universal idea of a triangle. Instead, claims Berkeley, the truth can be

---

[19] Chapter 2, section 2, pp. 14–17.

demonstrated on a particular triangle (a diagram, for example), and then extended to all triangles by omitting irrelevant facts about the particular triangle (its colour, for example).

One immediate problem with this view is how we determine in advance what is relevant or irrelevant. How does Berkeley know that, for example, the angles do not vary when the area of the triangle is increased or decreased? It is not clear that his account allows us to decide in advance what we can omit from the particular from which the generalisation is made. Putting that to one side, while we can agree that Berkeley's observation that the significance of a term is often determined by conventional rules is a true and interesting one,[20] one might wonder if he is failing to address an issue to which Locke claimed, perhaps optimistically, to have an answer. Locke appealed to abstract ideas in an effort to *explain* how we acquire the ability to classify things. Berkeley claims, correctly of course, that we do have that ability, but he does not explain how we have it.

We noted that Berkeley thinks philosophers are mistaken in their assumption that 'every significant name stands for an idea'. This mistake is compounded by a further one, namely, the 'received opinion, that language has no end but the communicating our ideas' (PHK I §19). This again is a view that can be attributed with some plausibility to Locke and amounts to the following:[21] by themselves words are just marks or noises and are not intrinsically *about* anything. They are conventional signs that, when heard or read, bring to mind the ideas with which they have become associated, and ideas in turn are about, or represent, objects. In learning the English language, I come to learn the conventional associations between, say, the words 'cat' and 'dog' and the relevant ideas, so that when I hear or see the words they suggest to me the ideas that represent dogs or cats. Words can be combined into complexes to form sentences, which can suggest particular collections of ideas that are representations of actual or possible facts. The sentence 'the cat is on the mat' suggests the collection of ideas that represents the cat on the mat, and is true when the cat is on the mat or false if the cat is not. When I utter the sentence 'the cat is on the mat' I communicate to you the fact that

[20] It figures greatly in his philosophy of mathematics, see Chapter 7, section 4, pp. 128–131.
[21] See Chapter 2, section 2, pp. 14–17.

the cat is on the mat, a fact that you understand when my words suggest to you the right ideas.

Now, Berkeley thinks that language does, indeed, sometimes function in this way, but 'the communicating of ideas marked by words is not the chief and only end of language' (PHK I §20). Language also serves in 'the raising of some passion, the exciting to, or deterring from an action, the putting the mind in some particular disposition' (PHK I §20). The basic point here is that often, when we use sentences in talking to others, our primary aim may be something other than communicating information. If I say to you 'you are late', my intention might not be to communicate that fact (you may indeed already know that), but instead to admonish you, arousing in you the emotion of guilt. Sat in the passenger seat of the car, I might say 'the light is green', exciting you to drive on. Or I might say 'Auntie is here', to encourage you to be on your best behaviour. Such utterances are different forms of 'speech act' where, as the philosopher J. L. Austin put it, 'in saying something, we do something'.[22] *Understanding* the speaker is not always simply a matter of understanding the conventional meaning of the sentence uttered, but also understanding the intention that the utterer is trying to convey by using the sentence.

For Berkeley, understanding the meaning of an utterance might involve the ideas the words used bring to mind. So when I say 'the light is green', the sentence might suggest in your mind the associated ideas and then you drive off. But for Berkeley the ideas suggested by words in the sentence can be 'barely subservient' to the aim in uttering it (PHK I §20). Furthermore, he suggests that in many cases the relevant ideas can be 'entirely omitted'. I am so used to your saying 'you are late' that its utterance elicits in me the feeling of guilt without my having to think, or have the ideas, that compose the thought 'I am late'. As Berkeley puts it in the draft introduction, 'it will be found that when language is once grown familiar to a man, the learning of the sounds or sight of the characters is oft immediately attended with those passions, which are first were wont to be produc'd, by the intervention of ideas that are now quite omitted'.[23] As long as the

---

[22] J. L. Austin, *How to Do Things with Words*, 2nd edn, ed. J. O. Urmson and Marina Sbisà (Cambridge, MA: Harvard University Press, 1975), p. 109.
[23] *Works*, vol. 2, p. 139.

hearer reacts in the way the speaker intends – he feels the appropriate passion, takes the right action or is put in to the right disposition – the hearer is said to 'understand perfectly' what is said:

For what is it I pray to understand perfectly, but only to understand all that is meant by the person who speaks? Which very oft is nothing more than barely to excite in his mind certain emotions without any thought of those ideas so much talk'd of and so little understood.[24]

At first sight these remarks about the ends of language, interesting and true though they are, seem entirely gratuitous. Their connection to the topic of abstract ideas seems somewhat tenuous. So why are these remarks here? The answer lies in the use that Berkeley makes of this claim later. He holds that what we take to be causal relations among natural events are actually relations of *signification*. Fire, for example, does not *cause* pain, but instead fire is a *sign* that warns of impending pain. For Berkeley, the relations among natural events constitute a language by means of which God is communicating with us. So when God causes in us the idea of fire – a sign for pain – we immediately get the idea of pain. But in so talking to us, God's intention is not merely to communicate ideas. The world is organised providentially, and God is speaking to us in order to inform us about what to *do* to flourish. The presence of a fire is a warning not to come too close, and we *understand* that warning when we act appropriately. Once we agree with Berkeley that the chief function of language is not merely the communication of ideas, but in getting the hearer to feel and act appropriately, we are better prepared to understand how natural events constitute the language of God and how, despite not realising that this is so, we in some sense understand that language. This topic is pursued later in this book.[25]

6 CONCLUSION

Berkeley closes his Introduction with the following points. Some disputes in philosophy are purely verbal, premised on the mistaken belief in abstract ideas. One should, counsels Berkeley, attend to one's own ideas and not be misled by the language we use to express them

---

[24] *Works*, vol. 2, p. 140.   [25] See Chapter 7.

(PHK I §22). He notes that this is a difficult task, and that the difficulty is compounded by the fiction of abstract ideas (PHK I §23). Nevertheless, 'we need only draw the curtain of words, to behold the fairest tree of knowledge, whose fruit is excellent, and within the reach of our hand' (PHK I §24). Hence, he entreats his readers, at PHK I §25, to use the words in his work as 'the occasion of his thinking, and endeavour to attain the same train of thoughts in his reading, that I had in writing them'.

What the reader should carry forward from this chapter is the following. Philosophy is prone to mistake because of its failure to understand language, and, indeed, its tendency to be positively misled by it. One mistake is to think that the end of language is simply the communication of ideas. Another is that every significant word stands for an idea. This is the mistake that encourages the doctrine that there are abstract ideas. What makes an abstract idea abstract, and hence objectionable, is that it is an attempt to conceive an impossibility. It is this also that lies behind the philosophical nonsense of materialism and its attendant unnatural scepticism. I shall discuss these connections in Chapter 5, section 5. In the next chapter we shall examine Berkeley's central argument for immaterialism.

CHAPTER 4

The argument for immaterialism

I INTRODUCTION

The focus of this chapter is Berkeley's immaterialism. Immaterialism is the thesis that physical objects depend on being perceived for their existence. The term 'immaterialism' might make one think that Berkeley's central claim is a merely negative one. It might, that is, encourage one to think that all there is to Berkeley's view is the denial of material substance. Berkeley does, indeed, argue against material substance, and so among the reasons to accept Berkeley's system is the failure of the materialist alternative. But that is not how Berkeley presents matters; he argues *for* immaterialism and *then* attacks materialism.

Berkeley's central positive case for immaterialism can be glossed as follows. Physical objects are sensible objects, and sensible objects are nothing but collections of sensible qualities. Sensible qualities are ideas, and ideas are mind-dependent. Since physical objects are just collections of ideas, physical objects must be mind-dependent. Berkeley thinks he can prove the truth of immaterialism very quickly. By PHK §3 tells us that we can have 'intuitive' knowledge that the absolute existence of sensible objects 'without the mind' is 'perfectly unintelligible', and in PHK §7 he declares that from 'what has been said, it follows there is no other substance than *spirit*, or that which perceives'. Sadly, Berkeley's brevity in exposition cannot be matched by equal brevity in interpretation. Just *what* Berkeley means by terms such as 'perceived', 'perception-dependence', 'spirit' and 'idea' is not obvious at first glance, and commentators are still arguing about understanding even these fundamental concepts.

Our first task, after outlining the main argument in more detail, is to examine what he means by 'sensible object' and 'sensible quality'. These are concepts that cannot be understood without at the same time discussing Berkeley's conception of the perceptual relation. We will then discuss the claim that sensible qualities are perception-dependent. There are two broad ways to understand Berkeley's case for the mind-dependence of sensible qualities. One way is to read him as taking over from Locke the philosophical thesis that what we immediately perceive are subjective entities on a par with pains and tickles.[1] Read this way, the *Principles* offers a incomplete case for immaterialism. The case is incomplete because the work offers no argument that what is immediately perceived are Lockean ideas. We have to wait for Berkeley's *Dialogues* for an argument for the thesis that what is immediately perceived are mind-dependent ideas.[2] The second way to understand the *Principles* sees it as offering a case for the mind-dependency of what we immediately perceive. Berkeley argues that the very concept of a 'sensible quality' – the qualities that compose the objects that we see, hear, feel, taste, touch and smell – is the concept of something that is essentially and exhaustively an *appearance* and that no sense can be made of the existence of something that is an appearance, and, at the same time, is not an appearance *to* a mind. Slightly more precisely, Berkeley holds that we cannot understand what can be meant by saying that a sensible quality exists except in terms of its appearing to some mind. This is how we should understand Berkeley's famous dictum that the *esse* (the essence or being) of sensible objects is *percipi* (to be perceived). So Berkeley does not begin with the Lockean view of 'ideas' and turn physical objects into ideas. Instead, he argues that we shall come to see that, when we reflect upon what we can mean by 'sensible quality', sensible qualities must be mind-dependent and, hence, because of their necessary relation to the mind, are 'ideas'. This second view, though controversial, is the one favoured in this book. It is not peculiar to me. A number of different commentators defend versions of it.[3] As we shall see in a number of places, the differences between these two readings of mind-dependency profoundly affect how we understand immaterialism.

---

[1] Cf. Chapter 2, section 4, pp. 22–25.
[2] For a recent reading along these lines, see Georges Dicker, *Berkeley's Idealism* (Oxford University Press, 2011), ch. 4.
[3] Versions of this view go back to at least the nineteenth century. It is perhaps most often associated with the editors of Berkeley's works, A. A. Luce and T. E. Jessop, and it is outlined in the Introduction to volume 2 of *The Works of George Berkeley*. This view is often called realism.

2 THE ARGUMENT FOR IMMATERIALISM

Berkeley's argument for immaterialism can be outlined, using (mostly) his own words, as follows:

(1) The objects of human knowledge are either 'ideas actually imprinted on the senses' or those 'perceived by attending to the passions or operations of the mind' (PHK §1).

(2) These objects of knowledge comprise a range of sensible qualities that we associate with particular sensory modalities. Thus by 'sight I have the ideas of light and colours . . . by touch I perceive . . . hard and soft, heat and cold' (PHK §1).

(3) The names used in ordinary language for things, such as 'apple' or 'tree', refer to collections or 'congeries' of ideas. The name 'apple', for example, stands for a collection of qualities, namely, 'a certain colour, taste, smell, figure and consistence'. These qualities 'having been observed to go together, are accounted one distinct thing, signified by the name *apple*' (PHK §1).

(4) There are minds that know or perceive these ideas (PHK §2).

(5) Besides the thoughts, passions and ideas of imagination that cannot exist without a mind, it is 'no less evident that the various sensations or ideas imprinted on the sense, however blended or combined together (that is, whatever objects they compose) cannot exist otherwise than in a mind perceiving them' (PHK §3).

(6) We can gain intuitive knowledge of this last claim by attending to 'what is meant by the term *exist* when applied to sensible things' (PHK §3).

(7) What I mean when I say a sensible thing exists is that I perceive it or, when I am not perceiving it, 'I should say it existed, meaning thereby that if I was in the study I might perceive it; or that some other spirit does actually perceive it' (PHK §3).

(8) The objects of ordinary common sense, like houses, rivers and trees, are things perceived by sense and so are 'sensible objects' (PHK §4).

(9) That sensible objects have an existence distinct from being perceived involves 'a manifest contradiction'. Sensible objects are the things perceived by sense and what we perceive by sense are [our] 'own ideas or sensations', which cannot exist unperceived (PHK §4).

Numerous complexities lurk beneath the surface of this seemingly simple argument. One group of questions that emerges from this argument centres on ideas and mind-dependency. Why does Berkeley hold (1),[4] and how does that relate to what he says in (5)? How is the claim in (5) supported by what is stated in (6) and (7)? Berkeley's claim (4), that there are minds or spirits, seems straightforward, but in fact conceals considerable difficulties that we shall not begin to unravel until Chapter 8. Item (8) contains the crucial claims that sensible objects are perceived by sense and what we perceive by sense is ideas. Sensible objects are those things that pre-philosophical common sense take to be *real things*, chairs, gloves, apples and oranges. This supposedly commonsensical view is then married with the philosophical claim that what is perceived by sense is ideas, and union is immaterialism. As Berkeley has Philonous say in the DHP, immaterialism unites the vulgar and the philosopher, the former believing that 'those things they immediately perceive are the real things' and the latter holding that 'the things immediately perceived, are ideas which exist only in the mind' (DHP3 262). Let us begin to explore things further by looking more closely at the notions of 'sensible object' and 'perception'.

3 THE SENSIBLE: OBJECTS, QUALITIES AND PERCEPTION

Berkeley offers us some examples of 'sensible objects' at PHK §4, namely, 'houses, mountains, rivers'. We have a fairly intuitive notion of the ordinary objects that we see, feel and touch on a day-to-day basis. Sensible objects are also identical to the things perceived by sense. What does Berkeley understand by 'perceived by sense'?

In some of his other writings, such as *An Essay Towards a New Theory of Vision* and the DHP, Berkeley draws a distinction between *immediate* and *mediate* perception. Only immediate perception is properly perceived by sense. The first, and uncontroversial, mark of immediate perception is that it is *passive*. I can be active when I perceive in the sense that I can turn my head to see something, but

---

[4] Berkeley does not in fact believe (1) if it is understood to mean that as well as sensible ideas we have ideas of the 'passions and the operations of the mind'. See Chapter 8, section 3, pp. 140–147 for further discussion of this point.

what I see when I turn my head is not down to me. Turning my head simply puts me in a position to 'receive' the experience, and in this sense I am passive when I perceive.[5] Secondly, immediate perception is a form of *conscious awareness*. Thirdly, it implies the existence of an object of awareness: there must be *something* of which you are consciously aware when you are aware. 'That a thing should be really perceived by my senses, and at the same time not really exist, is to me a plain contradiction' (DHP3 230). Finally, we are infallible with respect to that which we immediately perceive. It is a 'manifest contradiction to suppose' one 'should err in respect' of what we immediately perceive (DHP3 238).

The immediacy of immediate perception can be brought out by contrasting it with mediate perception. The basic idea of mediate perception is that when one mediately perceives *y*, the perception of idea *x* brings to mind the idea *y*. In that way, one can be said to perceive *y* by perceiving *x*. Thus:

> when the mind perceives any idea, not immediately . . . it must be by the means of some other idea . . . the passions which are in the mind of another are of themselves to me invisible. I may nevertheless perceive them by sight; though not immediately yet by means of the colours they produce in the countenance.[6]

So I 'see' someone's embarrassment *via* my immediate perception of the blush on his cheek; *y* is mediately perceived by my immediately perceiving *x*, *x* being the medium between *y* and me. In the example above one is *inferring* the embarrassment from the immediate perception of the colour on the cheek. Inference is a matter of conscious activity that one does on the basis of rules or principles. To infer embarrassment from a blush would involve consciously thinking people who have that colour on their cheeks tend to be embarrassed, so that person is probably embarrassed. A second way in which mediate perception operates is by an idea 'suggesting' another idea. Suggestion is not a conscious process, but instead a matter of what one immediately perceives straightaway bringing to mind other ideas, a

---

[5] Matters are, in fact, a little more complicated than they might seem. See below, Chapter 8, section 3.

[6] *An Essay Towards a New Theory of Vision*, §9, in *Works*, vol. 1, pp. 172–3.

link forged by habit, and reinforced by repeated experience. Berkeley
writes:

> To perceive is one thing; to judge is another. So, likewise to be suggested is
> one thing, and to be inferred is another. Things are suggested and perceived
> by sense. We make judgments and inferences by the understanding.[7]

So inference involves a conscious awareness of the evidential connections between ideas, whereas suggestion is an automatic *psychological*
process where ideas come to mind without involving the subject's
conscious thought. It is a matter of mental habit.

Immediate perception is not mediate perception. It involves no
inference and no intermediate idea. Immediate perception, as I mentioned, also enables the mind to have *infallible* knowledge of the
object immediately perceived. One cannot 'err' with respect to one
'perceives immediately and at present' (DHP3 238).[8] However, it is
important to note that immediate perception is not *itself* to know or
judge something. We sometimes say that we see or perceive *that*, for
example, it is raining. Such expressions interpret perception not
merely as a source of information, but as a form of immediate or
non-inferential *knowledge* or, less demandingly, *judgement*. When we
perceive *that* it is raining, we do not first see water drops *and* then
come to the conclusion that it is raining: we simply 'see' that it is
raining. For Berkeley, by contrast, immediate perception and judgement are two quite separate things. The infallibility owes itself to the
sheer cognitive intimacy of the object perceived and the perceiver.
The object is simply 'present to the mind' in such a way that it is
impossible for the subject to make a mistake over what she or he is
immediately perceiving.[9]

What do we immediately perceive? Berkeley talks of sensible qualities
and objects as combinations of sensible qualities, and he sometimes
suggests that sensible objects are immediately perceived. Thus:

> Wood, stones, fire, water, flesh, iron and the like things, which I name and
> discourse of, are things I know. And I should not have known them, but that

---

[7] *A New Theory of Vision Vindicated*, §42, in *Works* vol. 1, p. 265.
[8] 'Immediate perception also involves transparency.' This is the thesis that there is nothing more
to the object of immediate perception than is revealed in perception, but I propose to discuss
this below in section 4 when we discuss ideas.
[9] See further Chapter 8, section 2, pp. 133–140 on the activity involved in perception.

I perceived them by my senses; and things perceived by the senses are immediately perceived. (DHP3 230)

However, there are some texts suggesting that it is *not* these items that are the objects of immediate perception. There are, in other words, texts that seem to imply that, strictly speaking, we only immediately perceive the sensible *qualities* that compose those objects. Consider, for example, a discussion from the *Dialogues* around the perception of a coach. Suppose you are standing in a courtyard and you hear the sound that is typically made by coach. Do you hear the coach? In 'truth and strictness' Philonous says, 'nothing can be *heard* but *sound*: and the coach is not then properly perceived by sense, but suggested from experience' (DHP1 204). We hear the sound and, because we have associated the sound with coaches, we mediately perceive a coach by calling up those associated ideas. But given that immediate perception is contrasted with mediate perception, in the form of both inference and suggestion, it seems that ordinary objects are not immediately perceived. Instead, we immediately perceive sensible qualities, like particular colours or shapes, or particular sounds or smells, which in turn enter into the composition of objects likes rivers, trees and houses. Thus, Philonous asks Hylas whether 'we immediately perceive by sight any thing beside light, and colours, and figures: or by hearing, any thing but sounds: by the palate, any thing besides taste: by smell, besides odours; or by touch, more than tangible qualities' (DHP1 175). Hylas does not demur.

We can leave the issue of whether we immediately perceive qualities or objects to one side for the time being (we shall return to it at Chapter 6, section 6). What certainly *are* objects of immediate sense perception are sensible qualities. Since these compose ordinary objects, and since these are mind-dependent (for reasons discussed below), Berkeley can secure the mind-dependence of ordinary objects. Sensible qualities are the immediate objects of sense. What, then, are sensible qualities? Sensible qualities are those qualities that are distinguished by their respective and distinctive sensuous characters. Such qualities include colours, smells and tastes, and all others 'actually imprinted on the senses' (PHK §1). These qualities are such that one can only fully understand what these qualities are by experiencing them. To borrow an example from David Hume, I do not fully understand the taste of a pineapple unless I have actually tasted it: 'We cannot', he writes, 'form a just idea of the taste of a pine-apple, without actually having tasted it.'[10] You can tell me that it is a little like a sour melon, but that will not really convey to me everything about the peculiar taste of a pineapple that differentiates its taste from that of sour melon. Even then I am only in a position to know that pineapple tastes a little like melon because I have, and have exercised, the capacity to experience that taste of other things. Compare some-one who is colour-blind in the sense that all they experience is various shades of grey.[11] Since that person cannot experience chromatic colour, he or she not only does not fully understand redness, and has no understanding of what redness is *like* (we cannot, for example, tell him or her that it is a bit like brown, since he or she cannot experience that either). He or she may know *that* there are red things in the world, but lacks the capacity to have the peculiar experience that reveals what redness is like.

These qualities, according to Berkeley, are the qualities that com-pose physical objects. In PHK §1 he tells us that names used by ordinary language ('mountain', 'house', etc.) refer to collections or 'congeries' of these qualities. The term 'apple' does not pick out a collection of qualities whose unity is independent of the mind. Instead, the term 'apple' expresses a grouping together, or selection of, some qualities from among the total collection of qualities we perceive, a selection or grouping that owes itself to human interests. We could, if we wanted, group the qualities composing the apple with the qualities composing a tree to form a single object (a 'trapple'). A Lockean philosopher might see nothing objectionable here. How we sort things into kinds is in terms of a 'nominal essence', the collection of ideas associated with a particular name;[12] we human beings carve up or categorise these qualities into bundles to which we give familiar names like 'apple' or 'tree', and these collections 'constitute', say, the apple or the tree, or a particular 'sensible thing'. We shall return to this

---

[10] David Hume, *A Treatise of Human Nature*, ed. L. A. Selby-Bigge, rev. P. H. Nidditch (Oxford: Clarendon Press, 1978), p. 5.

[11] Genuine clinical colour blindness is a good deal more complex than this, and I simplify matters for the sake of getting the point across.

[12] See Chapter 2, section 3, pp. 17–22. For Locke, however, the unity of any group of sensible qualities is, in the final analysis, determined independently of the mind.

bundle theory of objects at a later stage.[13] For the time being let us note that the mind-dependence of sensible objects – trees, rivers and mountains – rests on the mind-dependency of the sensible qualities that constitute them. It is the mind-dependence of sensible qualities to which we now turn.

4 THE MIND-DEPENDENCE OF THE SENSIBLE: TWO READINGS

Why does Berkeley think that sensible qualities are mind-dependent? And in what sense are they mind-dependent?

As mentioned at the beginning of this chapter, commentators read Berkeley in one of two broad ways. The first sees him simply taking over uncritically the Lockean thesis that direct objects of perception are ideas.[14] What is meant by an 'idea' is the following. All sensory experience involves mental objects that consist of a collection of sensations that are akin to pains and tickles. It is these that are ideas, and they are 'private' or 'subjective' objects in the sense that they exist only in the particular minds of those experiencing them. Ideas are mind-dependent in that they, just like pains, exist only when being experienced. Since real objects are the immediate objects of sense, and the immediate objects of sense are mind-dependent in they way that pains are, real things are mind-dependent. Hence:

(9) That sensible objects have an existence distinct from being perceived involves 'a manifest contradiction'. Sensible objects are the things perceived by sense and what we perceive by sense are [our] 'own ideas or sensations', which cannot exist unperceived. (PHK §4)

Call this reading the 'ideas as sensations' (IS) reading. A number of things are in its favour. The first is that Berkeley appears to be working in the framework of the 'way of ideas' from the very first sentence of the main body of the *Principles*. He tells us that it is 'evident' that among the objects of human knowledge are 'ideas actually imprinted on the senses' (PHK §1). Surely he would talk about *objects* perceived, rather than ideas, if he was not taking over Locke's position? Secondly, he talks about 'sensations' when mounting his argument. Thus, at

PHK §3 he talks about 'various *sensations* or ideas imprinted on the senses', and again at PHK §4, as well as in numerous other places. Thirdly, in the *Dialogues* Philonous tells Hylas that he is attempting to reconcile the vulgar and the philosophers, the former holding that 'those things they immediately perceive are real things', and with the later that 'the things immediately perceived are ideas which exist only in the mind' (DHP3 262). It is quite natural to read this as a reference to an established philosophical position, and probably Locke's.

The IS reading, however, suffers from a serious weakness. Berkeley does not anywhere in the *Principles* offer any argument for the crucial premise that the immediate objects of sense are Lockean ideas. At best Berkeley's arguments will have any force only for those already persuaded of the 'way of ideas'. If one is unpersuaded by the Lockean way of ideas then Berkeley's *Principles* has no force.

It might be replied that this does not matter. Berkeley's DHP *does* provide such arguments, so the reply goes, and we should treat the fact that Berkeley provides no argument to accept the 'way of ideas' in the *Principles* as evidence that the text is a case of preaching to the converted. However, it is questionable that the arguments of the *Dialogues* should be read that way but, before we turn to this issue, let us consider our second way of reading the mind-dependence of sensible qualities in the *Principles*, one that does not rest on some prior assumption of the Lockean way of ideas. I shall call this the EP interpretation in honour of the famous claim made in PHK §3 that the *esse* of sensible objects is *percipi*, or that the essence of sensible objects is to be perceived. Note first, that although Berkeley tells us in PHK §3 that the ideas 'imprinted on the sense ... cannot exist otherwise than in a mind perceiving them', he does not *merely* tell us this. He also seems to be presenting an argument in favour of it, albeit in a very compressed fashion.[15] He claims that we are able to gain 'intuitive knowledge' of the truth that whatever objects which are composed by sensible qualities 'cannot exist otherwise than in a mind perceiving them' by considering the meaning of 'exists' when applied to sensible things. Now, if the opening sections simply assume that the objects of knowledge are ideas in the Lockean sense, then there

---

[15] It is not hard to feel sympathy with Kenneth Winkler who writes that PHK §3 seems 'not so much an argument as a series of assertions' (*Berkeley*, p. 175).

would be no need to argue that ideas cannot exist otherwise in the mind perceiving them. That is part and parcel of the claim that ideas are sensations. As Georges Dicker puts it, the claim that ideas (if ideas are sensations) cannot exist unperceived is 'obvious without *any* reflection on the meaning of the word "exists". No considerations about the meaning of "exist" are needed or even relevant to verify or justify the claim that an *idea* cannot exist unperceived.'[16]

However, there are uses of the term 'idea' that do not imply that ideas cannot exist unperceived. If Berkeley means 'idea' in *this* sense, then it makes sense to view what he says about the meaning of 'exist' as an argument that ideas are mind-dependent. But what sense of 'idea' is there which would not make ideas necessarily mind-dependent? One sense of 'idea' is a way of referring to what is 'before' the mind when one thinks or perceives. Thus Locke himself initially defines an idea as whatsoever 'the Mind perceives in itself, or is the immediate object of Perception, Thought or Understanding',[17] and Berkeley notes this use in the DHP when Philonous tells us 'idea . . . is now commonly used by philosophers, to denote the immediate objects of the understanding' (DHP3 236). This sense of 'idea' does *not* imply that perceptual ideas – the immediate objects of perception – are mind-dependent. Suppose you are looking at a cup. What is immediately before the mind is the surface of the cup, its colour and shape. These properties constitute what is the object of you perception and constitute what you perceive – they constitute your idea. If I turn the cup a little, your idea changes because what is before your mind is a different set of properties (you can no longer see the handle, for example). Your 'idea' of the cup is constituted by whatever properties of that cup are present to your mind. But that does not mean that the idea is some *mental* 'thing' that is distinct from the properties of the cup before your mind. The term 'idea' simply refers to what properties are perceived by the subject. Those properties are 'in the mind' only in the humdrum sense that they are things you are perceiving. We perceive those properties – we have those ideas – but the fact that they are 'in mind' when we perceive them does not imply that they *only* exist when they are perceived. The properties

[16] Dicker, *Berkeley's Idealism*, p. 70.   [17] E 2.8.8.

before the mind (which constitute our idea of the cup) continue to exist when we cease to look at them.

Perceived properties of objects are not the only things that are the immediate objects of the mind. The term 'idea' covers not merely what is perceived, but also what is thought, imagined, remembered, etc. It is easy to see why one might see this wider class of ideas as existing only in the mind in the sense of being mental entities, because it is plausible to hold that what we can think or imagine things that do not really exist. If there must be some thing that is the immediate object of thought when we think of things that do not exist (such as unicorns), we might then think that thing before the mind is some sort of mental entity that represents unicorns.[18] Berkeley, in PHK §3, takes it as evident that these ideas cannot exist without the mind. But given a sense of 'idea' as the immediate object of perception he needs an argument to support the claim ideas of sense – what we immediately perceive – 'cannot exist otherwise than in a mind perceiving them' (PHK §3). When the surface of the cup is perceived it is 'in the mind' and constitutes what the mind perceives, but that does not imply the surface of the cup cannot exist unperceived. Such things are the 'objects of knowledge' (PHK §1) because they are what is presented to the mind via perception (or 'imprinted on the senses').

So what is the argument? We gain knowledge that sensible things cannot exist without the mind by reflecting on 'what is meant by the term *exist* when applied to sensible things' (PHK §3). Reflection reveals that we cannot conceive of the existence of a sensible thing without its being perceived: 'There was an odour, it was smelled; there was a sound, that it is to say it was heard; a colour or figure, and it was perceived by sight or touch. This is all that I can understand by these and the like expressions.' The central thought is that any sensible quality is necessarily a form of *appearance*, and, crucially, we cannot make sense of the existence of any appearance without it appearing *to* a mind. The slogan 'to be is to be perceived' is to be interpreted as the claim that for a sensible thing to exist is for it to *appear* to a mind. Hence, what is to be a sensible quality is necessarily to be perceived. On the EP interpretation, the argument for the mind-dependence of sensible qualities does not rest on some presupposed Lockean thesis

---

[18] Compare Chapter 3, section 4, pp. 45–49.

about ideas as sensations, but instead rests on identifying sensible qualities with appearances and the intuition that appearances cannot exist without the minds for which they are appearances. It is a contradiction to say that there is an appearance – a colour or an odour – that exists when it does not appear *to* anyone.

This provides an intuitive argument for the mind-dependence of sensible qualities. It means that the PHK provides an argument for mind-dependency of what is immediately perceived that is absent on the IS reading. It accords well with the importance Berkeley places on the idea of existence in the *Philosophical Commentaries*. For example, he writes that 'the Discovering of the nature & meaning & import of Existence that I chiefly insist. This puts a wide difference betwixt the Sceptics & me. This I think wholly new. I am sure 'tis new to me' (PC 491). But two worries about its effectiveness immediately spring to mind. The argument trades on the thought that all we understand by a sensible object is a characteristic appearance, and that we cannot understand an appearance existing and yet not appearing to some mind. But this seems false on two grounds.

First, we do not think of objects as *merely* forms of appearance. I do not think the book on my desk is exhausted by how it appears now. I think, for example, that there is more to it than I presently see (it has a back cover, for example). I also think that objects can seem otherwise than they really are. A red object can appear blue under abnormal lighting conditions. Berkeley has answers to these objections as we shall see, but the immediate problem is that if these claims are part of what we understand by 'sensible object', then the argument for mind-dependency cannot get off the ground.[19] But Berkeley's strategy here is subtle. The mind-dependency of a sensible object is a consequence of the claim that objects are collections of immediately perceived sensible *qualities* and sensible qualities cannot be conceived to exist except as a form of appearance. That is why in PHK §3 he mentions qualities like colour and odour. We might be able to distinguish between an object's looking red and its being red, but it is rather more difficult to distinguish *redness* from its appearing red. To be red is just to appear red. So Berkeley gets the mind-dependence of objects from their being composed of mind-dependent qualities; but we

[19] See Chapter 6, section 6, pp. 104–114.

should leave aside at this stage the distinctions we want to draw between the way *objects* seem and how they really are.

This brings us to the second objection. Surely we can understand the existence of a sensible quality or appearance when no one is perceiving it? When the washing machine is going in the apartment while I am at work I am not there to smell its characteristic odour, but I can understand that my apartment still smells that way. One way to express this thought is that the smell continues to exist when I cease to perceive it. How is that possible? One answer is to say that although the odour is not actually smelled we can make sense of its continued existence by saying that it exists because it is *perceivable*. There seems to be no sense attached to the claim that there is a smell that no one could ever smell, or a colour that no one could ever see. At the very least every sensible object must be *perceivable*. Perhaps Berkeley should not claim that the *esse* of a sensible quality is *percipi* or be perceived, but instead their *esse est percipi aut posse percipi*: the essence of sensible qualities is to be perceived or perceivable. To be is either to appear to a mind or at least be the *possibility* of appearance.

This more liberal view would still secure mind-dependence in the sense that sensible qualities cannot exist except as actual or possible appearances. It is consistent with Berkeley's denial of absolute existence of 'unthinking things [*sic* sensible qualities] without any relation to their being perceived' (PHK §3). There is a hint of this view in PHK §3 when Berkeley says that 'when not actually perceiving the table in the study I should say it existed, meaning that if I was in the study I might perceive it'. Such a view is called 'phenomenalism' and holds that what we mean by a given object is a collection of actual or possible appearances. As we shall see in Chapter 6, section 3, this is not Berkeley's view. Berkeley holds that since sensible qualities are essentially appearances, they must be perceived to exist. But what of the point above, namely, that I can make sense of a smell unperceived by me? There is a different answer to this objection hinted at in PHK §6 where Berkeley says that 'since the being . . . [of sensible objects] is to be perceived or known . . . they must either have no existence at all, or else subsist in the mind of some eternal spirit'. Sensible qualities, appearances, are independent of me, but sustained by God's perception. Reality is sustained by its consisting in appearance for God and those appearances are independent of finite spirits like you or me. How we are to understand this claim is taken up in Chapter 6, section 3.

What, then, of the arguments for mind-dependence Berkeley offers in the *Dialogues*? Do they support the IS or the EP interpretation? There are two broad strategies offered in the First Dialogue. One is what is known as the 'assimilation argument' and is found at various places, but primarily DHP1 175–80. The argument can be expressed as follows, using one of Berkeley's own examples. Heat is a sensible quality, and, like all sensible qualities, it comes in degrees. Intense heat is painful, and what we immediately perceive in such a case is not two distinct sensations, but a single uniform sensation of intense, painful heat. Intense heat is a form of pain, pain is evidently mind-dependent, and so intense heat is mind-dependent. But the only relevant difference between intense heat and heat is merely one of degree, and differences in degree do not make for differences in *kind*. So if intense heat is mind-dependent, then *all* degrees of heat are mind-dependent (DHP1 175–80). The sensible qualities that fall under our sense of taste are all either forms of pleasure or pain (DHP1 180). The second strategy Berkeley employs is a series of conflicting appearance arguments (DHP 180–7). In outline the form of such arguments runs as follows.[20] Any object can appear in different ways under different circumstances. A shirt can appear blue in daylight, but purple under the lights in the bar. Under which conditions is the 'real' colour of the shirt revealed? There is no non-arbitrary way of deciding whether it is 'really' blue or 'really' purple. So, the thought goes, it is a mistake to think that there is such a thing as the real colour of the object. Colour is consigned to the 'appearance' side of the reality and appearance divide. This strategy is then generalised to *every* sensible quality, so that every sensible quality is identified with a 'quality in the mind'.

Now, it is beyond the scope of this book to examine these arguments, but two points are to be made here. First, many of these arguments are directed against the notion of material substance rather than constituting an argument for immaterialism. Secondly, and importantly, the arguments are offered in service of the EP principle. Philonous wanted to dissuade Hylas of his belief that we can

---

[20] See also Chapter 5, section 3, pp. 74–77.

distinguish the existence of sensible objects from their being perceived. Thus:

PHILONOUS: Doth the reality of sensible things consist in being perceived? or, is it something distinct from their being perceived, and that bears no relation to the mind?
HYLAS: To *exist* is one thing, to be *perceived* is another.

(DHP1 175)

5 CONCLUSION

Berkeley writes that from what he has said it follows that:

all the choir of heaven and the furniture of the world, in a word all those bodies which compose the mighty frame of the world, have not any subsistence without a mind, that their being is to be perceived or known ... To be convinced of which, the reader need only reflect and try to separate in his own thoughts the being of a sensible thing from its being perceived. (PHK §6)

Houses and trees are sensible objects, and sensible objects are collections of sensible qualities. Sensible qualities are mind-dependent. Therefore, houses and trees and all sensible objects are mind-dependent. There are two interpretations of Berkeley's argument for mind-dependence of sensible qualities in the PHK. One is that he simply assumes his reader will agree that the immediate objects are mind-dependent ideas and needs only to be persuaded of the identification of houses, trees and so on with the immediate objects of sense. This is the IS interpretation. The EP interpretation, on the other hand, rests on the idea that sensible quality is necessarily perceived or at least perceivable. We can give no sense to the thought that there exists a sensible quality that has an 'absolute existence without the mind'. While we cannot decide which interpretation is ultimately the correct one until we have considered more of Berkeley's system, the drift of the discussion has been in favour of the second interpretation of the argument for mind-dependence. Furthermore, we need to consider whether Berkeley's system leaves any room for the existence of unperceived sensible objects. Both these matters are cleared up in Chapter 6. Chapter 6 will also show that the mind-dependence of objects does not prevent us from having a robust account of the real world.

CHAPTER 5

Against the philosophers: the refutation of materialism

I INTRODUCTION

The previous chapter discussed Berkeley's case for immaterialism. The basis for this idea is a claim about the essence of sensible qualities. A sensible quality is essentially a form of appearance, and so it exists only in relation to a mind. The physical objects that populate the world are just collections of these sensible qualities and so physical objects are mind-dependent.

Much of the *Principles* attempts to show how this central insight is consistent with what we ordinarily believe of the world and how we are to understand the practice of science in its light. However, Berkeley's first move, after offering his case for immaterialism, is to dispose of materialism. His objections to materialism are the subject of the present chapter. He has a battery of different objections to different characterisations of material substance, treating it, as Kenneth Winkler aptly puts it, as 'a moving target'.[1] This is not a surprise. As we saw in Chapter 2 there are differing views on material substance, and so Berkeley considers a different version of the doctrine and possible responses to his objections.

In this chapter we shall, for the most part, follow the order in which Berkeley presents his criticism in the text. The first criticism, discussed in section 2, turns on the claim that ideas cannot resemble anything but ideas. If this is so, the Lockean account of how we represent material objects is impossible, since it rests on the supposition of a resemblance between ideas and material objects. The second criticism, taken up at section 3, is that the distinction between primary

---

[1] Winkler, *Berkeley: An Interpretation*, p. 178.

and secondary qualities, so central to the doctrine of material sub-stance, is unsustainable. Here Berkeley again raises the topic of abstract ideas, but, as we shall see, these sections do not get to the bottom of the mystery of the connection between materialism and abstraction. In section 4, we discuss some further criticisms of material substance, which include Berkeley's positing a dilemma whereby either the notion of material substance is incoherent or it is empty. On either horn of this dilemma the expression 'material substance' is meaningless. Section 5 finally identifies the relationship between abstraction and materialism. The final section, section 6, discusses a sequence of thoughts Berkeley expresses at PHK §§22–3 that have become known as Berkeley's 'master argument' for imma-terialism.[2] This labelling is shown to be a doubly ironic mistake. The first irony is that if there is an argument here, then, far from being a master argument, it is a very poor one indeed. The second irony is the fact these sections are not intended as an *argument* for immaterialism at all. It is simply a challenge to the reader, the effectiveness of which rests on Berkeley's prior case for immaterialism.

2 IDEAS AND RESEMBLANCE (PHK §8)

In PHK §8, Berkeley anticipates an objection to his account that would occur to any Lockean philosopher. Of course, the immediate objects of sense – ideas – do not exist without the mind. But those ideas *represent* mind-independent objects by the relation of resem-blance. Chairs and tables, which exist independently of perceivers, are not the immediate objects of sense, but the things represented by ideas. Sensory ideas, then, are perceptual representations of objects and their qualities.

Although Berkeley does not use the term 'material substance' in this section, it is clearly presupposed. The sensible qualities that ideas purportedly represent are supposed to exist independently of the mind and inhere in material substance. Berkeley counters this claim by asserting that it is 'possible for us to conceive a likeness only between our ideas'. There cannot be a relation of likeness or

---

[2] The term 'master argument' was coined by André Gallois in his paper, 'Berkeley's Master Argument', *Philosophical Review* 83 (1974), 55–69.

resemblance between an idea and a mind-independent quality or object that the Lockean supposes and so ideas cannot represent material things by resembling them.

Unfortunately, Berkeley offers no justification in the *Principles* for what has become known as his 'Likeness Principle', the claim that only an idea can be like an idea. This failure to offer a defence of the Likeness Principle is compounded by the fact that Berkeley also fails to consider another way in which ideas might represent the qualities of material objects. As we saw in Chapter 2, section 5, Locke held that our ideas of secondary qualities represent those qualities in virtue of the fact that the former are regularly caused by the latter. Ideas are 'natural signs' for qualities. Berkeley ignores this possibility entirely. Let us first examine why Berkeley felt he could ignore the natural signs model before turning to the Likeness Principle itself.

One reason is that he is sceptical of the possibility of invoking matter to explain the production of our ideas (PHK §19). Though 'we give the materialists their external bodies, they by their own confession are never the nearer knowing how our ideas are produced: since they own themselves unable to comprehend in what manner body can act upon spirit, or how it is possible it should imprint any idea in the mind'. So, if we cannot really explain how it is possible for matter to cause ideas, the claim that ideas represent qualities because the former are regularly caused by the latter seems dubious. However, there is a deeper reason why Berkeley does not take the natural sign view worthy of explicit consideration in the *Principles*. It is quite true, and something Berkeley believes himself, that x can be used to represent y even though there is no resemblance relationship between x and y.[3] The word 'cat', for example, is used to represent cats, but it does not represent them by resembling them. What is more, we can, and do, take causal effects to be 'signs' for something else. For example, we say that spots are a sign of measles. But how can we say that something 'represents' something else if we are never in a position to tell *what* it is that it represents? Remember, the idea of a secondary quality represents whatever it is that regularly causes that idea, but in advance of scientific discovery of what that quality is the best we can say is that the idea is a representation of 'something' we do not

---

[3] See Chapter 7, section 2, pp. 117–121.

understand. Still, we might be happy, generally speaking, about allowing that an idea is a sign for 'something, though we know not what' if it is at least possible to discover what it is that is in fact a cause of that idea. Thus, to return to the measles example, I can suspect that the spots I have are a sign for something, but not know what it is. I need to ask the doctor, who tells me that such spots mean (are caused by) measles. Analogously, I might believe my idea of redness is a sign for some physical cause without knowing what that cause is, and defer to the scientist to inform what it is that my idea is an idea of. However, if no one could ever tell what is the cause of my idea, would it make sense to say that the idea is a *representation* or *sign* of a quality? How would something represent something else if one could never under-stand what that sign or representation *means*? That sounds completely implausible. So the claim that ideas of secondary qualities are natural signs for their causes only makes sense if we can, at least in principle, be in a position to understand just what qualities are the causes for those ideas. Here Locke will say that we can understand such causes because we can understand the primary qualities which are the causes of ideas. The success of this reply, however, rests on the assumption that we can represent primary qualities. To understand redness as an arrangement of primary qualities that causes the idea of red requires that we can gain some understanding of those qualities. This points us back to the resemblance or likeness thesis. To grasp what causes ideas in us we must be able to understand what the causal qualities are. Such understanding, for Locke, is furnished by the fact that not only are our ideas of primary qualities caused by those qualities, but our ideas *resemble* those qualities and so reveal what the natures of those qualities are. Without the Locke's resemblance thesis in place, we cannot represent the mind-independent qualities that supposedly cause the ideas of the secondary qualities.

What grounds, then, does Berkeley have for his Likeness Principle? One thought is that Berkeley assumes that for *x* to resemble *y*, *x* and *y* must share the same properties. He rejects the claim that we have an idea of *spirit*, he says that because the 'very being of an idea implies passiveness and inertness in it [. . . and so it cannot] be the resem-blance or pattern of any active being, as is evident from *Sect.* 8' (PHK §25). Ideas cannot represent an active being *because* they are passive. This suggests that resemblance requires property sharing, while the supposed resemblance between an idea and some mind-independent quality would fail because ideas are essentially perception-dependent and anything they resemble must be perception-dependent as well.

We do not, however, find in Berkeley's writings an explicit statement to the effect that resemblance requires property sharing. Entry 378 in the *Philosophical Commentaries* suggests a different reason why Berkeley thought his Likeness Principle was true. There he says that two 'things cannot be said to be alike or unlike until they have been compar'd'. The intuition here is that whether x is like y depends on whether we *judge* it to be so. But how is it possible to compare our ideas directly with 'external objects'? We cannot 'climb out of our minds' to look and see whether our ideas resemble external objects, because all our thought and experience of those objects is, on the Lockean view, mediated *by* ideas. So, since we cannot compare ideas with objects the two things cannot be said to be alike. This, then, is perhaps what lies behind Berkeley's claim that it is 'possible for us to conceive a likeness only between our ideas'.[4]

3 PRIMARY AND SECONDARY QUALITIES (PHK §§9–15)

Berkeley next turns to attack a central doctrine of the philosophy of material substance. This is the distinction between primary and secondary qualities. As we saw, both Locke and Malebranche, though in different ways, think that material substance is to be characterised fundamentally as consisting in primary qualities.[5] Matter is the 'inert, senseless substance in which extension, figure, and motion, do actually subsist'. All other qualities that are apparently perceived in objects are 'secondary'.

Berkeley's criticisms of the distinction between primary and secondary qualities are not themselves attempts to establish the truth of immaterialism. Instead, he is concerned to show that no such distinction can be maintained. This is important to him for three reasons. First, he thinks that the distinction is an affront to common sense. It implies that aspects of the physical world are systematically not as they seem to be.[6] Secondly, the supposed conceptions of material

---

[4] For a fuller discussion see Winkler, *Berkeley: An Interpretation*, pp. 141–8.
[5] Chapter 2, section 5, pp. 25–29.   [6] Chapter 2, section 5, pp. 25–29.

substance offered by Locke and Malebranche depend on their being able to make the distinction. Thirdly, the distinction affords Berkeley an *ad hominem* argument against the advocates of material substance. If the arguments that are supposed to show that colour, etc. are mind-dependent are shown to be applicable to *all* sensible qualities – including shape and extension – then Berkeley's opponents must hold that all qualities of bodies are mind-dependent.

Recall that in his discussion of abstract ideas Berkeley held that certain qualities are 'inseparably connected'. We cannot, for example, conceive any particular colour without its having some particular shape.[7] Every determinable of one quality is necessarily connected with a determinable of another. Thus, when it comes to an attempt to conceive extension I can conceive of it only in one of two ways: first, I can conceive it visually, but to do so I must conceive it as coloured in one way or another; secondly, I can conceive of extension by touch through the sensations I enjoy as I move my hand around, say, the surface of the table. Both colour and the sensations of touch are thought to be secondary qualities and thus mind-dependent. Yet if these are mind-dependent, and extension is inseparably connected with these qualities, then extension is mind-dependent. Thus, 'extension, figure, and motion, abstracted from all other qualities, are inconceivable. Where therefore the other sensible qualities are, there must be these also, to wit, in the mind and nowhere else' (PHK §10).

Although Berkeley objects to the distinction between primary and secondary qualities on the grounds that it requires an impossible feat of abstraction, this does not yet get to the bottom of the relation between abstraction and materialism, as we shall see.[8] There are two further features of the discussion in the PHK worth noting. First, Berkeley holds that the primary and secondary quality distinction implies that colours, smells, etc., are 'in the mind'. Secondly, he holds that the distinction is best supported by the Argument from Conflicting Appearances.[9] One and the same physical object can appear differently to the same person under different circumstances. For example, an object can look blue under sunlight, but violet under different lighting conditions. It is plausible to assume that it does not change colour when the

---

[7] Chapter 3, section 3, pp. 38–39.   [8] See below, section 5, pp. 79–82.
[9] Chapter 4, section 4, p. 68.

circumstances change. The question then arises: which circumstances reveal its 'real' colour? The problem is that we have no non-arbitrary way of determining *which* circumstances reveal the true colour of the object. The best response is to conclude that there is no 'real' or 'true', and colour is merely a mode of appearance or 'in the mind'. Berkeley's *ad hominem* point is that this argument can be generalised to all perceived qualities, including the so-called primary qualities, but, as he says, it 'must be confessed this method of arguing doth not so much prove that there is no extension or colour in an outward object, as that we do not know by sense which is the true extension or colour of the object' (PHK §15).

Now commentators claim that Berkeley's view that modern philosophy maintains that secondary qualities are 'in the mind' and that the argument for the distinction rests on the Argument from Conflicting Appearances show that he, once again, badly misreads Locke.[10] His secondary qualities are powers in objects, not perceptions in the mind.[11] Nor does Locke rely on an argument from Conflicting Appearances to support the distinction. However, this is false. Instead, these two features of his treatment of the primary and secondary qualities distinction shows that Berkeley understands the distinction in the light of Malebranche and Bayle. Both use the Argument from Conflicting Appearances for the distinction, and it is they that hold that colours are 'in the mind'; secondary qualities are merely sensations projected back onto material substance.[12] This view is motivated partly on the grounds that what we *mean* by 'colour' and other sensible qualities is their peculiar intrinsic qualitative character, and the new physics implies that the only bearers of these qualities are minds. This is how Berkeley understands qualities like colour, and why he thinks that the mechanical philosophy implies they are in the mind. He clearly knows the Lockean claim that colours are powers, because Hylas mentions, in this connection, the thesis that there are 'minute particles ... agitated with a brisk motion, and in various manners reflected from the different surfaces of objects ... [which are] attended with the sensation of red, blue, yellow, &c' (DHP1 186).

---

[10] See, e.g., Bennett, *Learning from Six Philosophers*, vol. 2, pp. 148–9. For a reading more sympathetic of Berkeley, see Margaret Wilson, 'Did Berkeley Completely Misunderstand the Basis of the Primary–Secondary Quality Distinction in Locke?', in *Ideas and Mechanism: Essays on Early Modern Philosophy* (Princeton University Press, 1999), pp. 215–28.

[11] See Chapter 2, section 5, pp. 25–29.   [12] Chapter 2, section 5, pp. 25–29.

However, like his French influences, Berkeley holds that the correct understanding of colours is that they are sensible qualities 'which are alone thought colours by all mankind', as Philonous puts it (DHP1 187). The claim that colours are 'certain unknown motions and figures which no man ever did or can see' is a 'shocking' one. The colours of materialist philosophy are rendered 'invisible'.

There is one more thing to note in Berkeley's discussion of the primary and secondary quality distinction, and this time it is right to think that Locke is in Berkeley's sights. Locke included 'number' as a primary quality and Berkeley objects to this at PHK §1, claiming that number has 'no absolute existence without the mind'. Berkeley also rejects the claim that we have an abstract idea of *unity* in PHK §13, whereas Locke thought the idea of unity was that simplest of all ideas, an idea of a thing with 'no shadow of Variety or Composition in it'.[13] Berkeley's claim is that there is no fact of the matter regarding the number of things there are until we decide what *counts* as a thing. This is a claim we shall take up when we discuss Berkeley's philosophy of arithmetic.[14]

4 MORE ATTACKS ON MATTER (PHK §§16–21)

Berkeley continues his attack on material substance with a rapid succession of objections. One of his most important is slipped in earlier (PHK §9), at the beginning of his discussion of the primary and secondary quality distinction. The very supposition of material substance is, he argues, incoherent. Material substance is supposed to be non-thinking or non-perceiving. It is also supposed to be that upon which sensible qualities depend. However, due reflection on the meaning of 'sensible quality' reveals that sensible qualities depend on perceivers for their existence. Material substance would, therefore, be the unperceiving thing upon which qualities that depend on perceivers for their existence are supposed to depend. Philosophers are not aware that the notion of material substance is incoherent, because they fail to recognise that sensible qualities are perceiver-dependent. Nevertheless, the material substance, so supposed, is incoherent.

---

[13] E 2.16.1.   [14] See Chapter 7, section 4, pp. 128–130.

This argument depends on Berkeley's making good his case for the perceiver-dependency of sensible qualities, and, if he is successful, it is a powerful objection to material substance. The materialist, however, might disavow this incoherent characterisation of material substance, but then he or she must try to provide some alternative meaning for the expression 'material substance'. The problem is that in trying to avoid incoherence the materialist is likely to fall into vagueness or emptiness. Thus, for example, trying to characterise material substance as 'being in general' seems hopelessly vague (PHK §17). Relatedly, the crucial notion of dependency needs to be given some meaning, and Berkeley attacks Locke on this score as well. Locke had claimed that matter is the 'unknown support' of qualities and that the 'true import of the Word [support], is in plain *English, standing under,* or *upholding'*.[15] Berkeley objects to this in PHK §16, and in particular the notion of 'support'. Surely Locke cannot mean support in the literal sense, like that of a chair supporting my body. The literal notion of 'support' makes no sense here. Locke could instead say that there is *some* kind of dependency relation, but we are owed an account of that relation.

These are short but powerful arguments. The use of words like 'material substance', 'inhere' and 'support' is no guarantee that there are meanings attached to them. A secondary battery of arguments proceeds by showing that, even if we grant some genuine meaning could be attached to the notion of material substance, there remain insuperable problems for it as a hypothesis. One problem, stated in PHK §18, is just how we can secure knowledge of its existence.[16] Perhaps one might argue that the existence of matter is required as the best explanation of the causation of ideas. However, as Berkeley points out, Locke himself confesses that he does not know *how* material objects can act upon minds. The materialists 'by their own confession . . . own themselves unable to comprehend in what manner body can act upon spirit' (PHK §19). So how can one invoke matter to explain why we have ideas if we do not know how matter causes ideas in us? The second half of PHK §19 then switches to Malebranche. As we saw, whereas Locke thought it difficult to understand how matter caused ideas, Malebranche positively denied that it causes them at all.

---

[15] E 2.23.3.   [16] Compare Chapter 2, section 4, pp. 22–25.

Instead, God causes sensations in us that help us to know external bodies. But now what role do bodies really play? They do not cause anything, and Malebranche himself said that their existence is a matter of 'faith'. As Berkeley puts it, Malebranche's God must create material objects that are 'entirely useless, and serve no manner of purpose'.

In sum: an unperceiving support for sensible qualities is actually a contradiction when we realise that sensible qualities are perception-dependent. Notions like 'unknown support' or 'being in general' seem empty. Even if there were such a thing, it would not really explain anything and we could not know it anyway. Berkeley's compact demolition of materials brings to the fore the inherent conceptual and epistemological doctrines in the notion of material substance in a forceful manner.

5 ABSTRACTION, COMMON SENSE AND IMMATERIALISM

Now to finish some unfinished business. How is it that the 'opinion strangely prevailing among men, that . . . sensible objects have existence . . . distinct from their being perceived' (PHK §4), 'depend on the doctrine of *abstract ideas*'? (PHK §5).

The first question is among whom is the 'opinion strangely prevailing'? It seems to me that Berkeley cannot mean among human beings in general, but only among philosophers. Why? Well, ordinary people not only do not have abstract ideas (because they are impossible, and no one has them), but also they do not even *think* they have them, according to Berkeley. Thus, at PC 703, Berkeley states that 'Abstract ideas [are] only to be had amongst the Learned. The Vulgar never think they have any such, nor truly do they find any want of them.' So the 'opinion strangely prevailing' must prevail only among philosophers. It is they that explicitly hold that sensible objects can exist unperceived, a mistaken view that rests on abstraction.

Before we examine how abstraction leads to this opinion, we need to say a little more about what Berkeley takes the ordinary or 'vulgar' attitude to the world to be. For, at first blush, what he says elsewhere might make it seem that everyone is of the 'opinion strangely prevailing' and not just philosophers. At PHK §56 he considers the 'prejudice' that 'objects of perception had an existence independent of, and without the mind'. This prejudice emerges because many ideas we have are not under the direct control of our will, and so we suppose them not dependent on our minds. This leads us to treat such ideas (things) as if they are not the direct effects of minds. But, crucially, Berkeley holds that acting this way is not the same thing as *believing* that sensible objects exist independently of the mind.

One reason for thinking that the vulgar do not believe that objects exist independently of perception is as follows. In PHK §56, Berkeley is responding to an objection that his theory implies that everyone in the world is radically mistaken. Everyone believes that objects exist independently of perceivers. But, Berkeley counters, 'upon a narrow inquiry, it will not perhaps be found, so many as is imagined do really believe in the existence of matter or things without the mind. Strictly speaking, to believe that which contains a contradiction, or has no meaning in it, is impossible' (PHK §54).

One mark of abstraction is the attempt to think the impossible. Philosophers believe that such impossible thoughts are in fact possible because they are mislead by language. The impossible thought in this case is that sensible qualities or sensible objects exist independently of perception. But what might mislead them into thinking that this is a genuine thought at all?

To appreciate how philosophers come to their mistaken opinion, we need to look in more detail at the vulgar 'prejudice' and how it differs from the philosophical opinion. To repeat what I said above, in responding to the objection that his theory imputes to ordinary common sense the widespread error that sensible objects exist unperceived, he tells us that 'upon a narrow inquiry, it will not perhaps be found, so many as is imagined do really believe the existence of matter or things without the mind. Strictly speaking, to believe that which contains a contradiction, or has no meaning in it, is impossible' (PHK §54). Berkeley holds, with some plausibility, that one can believe something is the case only when it is capable of being true. When we believe something there is something *that* we believe.[17] We believe *that* it is raining, *that* Lincoln Park Zoo is open, or *that* the post has arrived. What are referred to in the 'that' clause of belief statements are

---

[17] There is a different sense of belief, namely, that we can believe *in* something. This is, roughly, when we trust in, or rely on, something. But that is not the sense of belief operative here.

descriptions of the world as one way or another, descriptions that are true if the world is a particular way or false otherwise. Of course, that is not to say that everything we believe *is* true, but rather we can only believe something we can understand what it would be for it to be true. So the sentence 'Teddy is at school' is true just in case Teddy is at school or false otherwise. If Teddy is not at school, the sentence 'Teddy is at school' is false, but nevertheless it *could* be true inasmuch as what would make it true is readily intelligible. However, if Berkeley is right and there is a contradiction in the supposition of the unperceived existence of sensible objects, then there are no circumstances under which it is true that they exist unperceived. So any attitude we have to the sentence 'sensible objects exist independently of all minds' cannot be one of belief. This claim of Berkeley's is an important aspect of his thesis that immaterialism is not anti-common sense. Since no one ever genuinely *believed* in the absolute existence of sensible objects, Berkeley's claim that it is impossible that they so exist contradicts nothing we ordinarily believe.

Berkeley grants that the vulgar act in a certain way, which could be *called* belief. We 'act as if the immediate cause of their sensations . . . were some senseless unthinking being' (PHK §54). As a result, we behave as if ideas do not have a spirit as their cause, but Berkeley thinks that we will come to realise that this stance is inappropriate. The immediate cause of perceptual experience is God, and we should view perceptual experience as a system of signs.[18] But the presently inappropriate behaviour is just that: inappropriate behaviour, and not a belief about the metaphysical status of sensible objects.[19]

We also express this pseudo-belief with terms like 'material object' or 'matter' in ordinary talk. It is these words upon which philosophers fasten, and which engender the 'opinion strangely prevailing' of the philosophers in contradiction to the vulgar who do not form 'a settled speculative opinion' (PHK §56). The philosophers take such words to express a genuine belief in the perception-independent existence of

---

[18] See Chapter 7, section 2, pp. 117–121.
[19] In effect, Berkeley is turning a standard story of religious commitment on its head. Philosophers like Hume hold that religious belief emerges because we illegitimately treat natural events as the result of the intentional actions of invisible spirits, but we should properly regard those events as the blind consequence of mechanism. Berkeley thinks that this view has things back to front.

sensible qualities. The attempted philosophical articulation of this alleged belief culminates in the doctrine of material substance and its attendant complications. This is because it fixes upon words like 'material thing' and attempts to 'apprehend [some] meaning marked by these words, and form thereof a settle[d] speculative opinion'. But, in fact, philosophers only 'impose upon themselves, by imagining they believe those propositions they have often heard, though at bottom they have no meaning in them' (PHK §54). Why the interpretation rests on abstraction is because what makes any putative thought abstract is that it is a misguided attempt to *conceive what is impossible*. There is no 'nicer strain of abstraction than to distinguish the existence of sensible objects from their being perceived, so as to conceive them existing unperceived' (PHK §5). The expression 'material object' and the ways in which we behave encourage philosophers in thinking that behind this lies a genuine thought or idea that sensible objects exist unperceived, a thought expressed by an idea that would have to involve that abstraction of sensible object from perception. The 'unnatural doubts' engendered by the edifice of material substance rest entirely upon this illegitimate abstraction.[20]

We can now see the point of the critique of abstraction in the Introduction to the *Principles*. Berkeley wants to cure philosophers of the source of their mistaken attachment to materialism. Doing so does not, of course, constitute a reason to believe immaterialism, but it does show (if it succeeds) just where the philosophers go wrong, and so loosens the attachment they have to materialism. This also explains why Berkeley does not repeat his critique of abstract ideas in the DHP. The DHP is an attempt to convince an intelligent reader who is not married to a prior philosophical position of the truth of immaterialism. Hylas is not presented as a philosopher, and so has no philosophical diseases needing to be cured.

6 THE 'MASTER ARGUMENT'

At PHK §22 Berkeley says 'I am afraid I have given cause to think me needlessly prolix in handling the subject'. Perhaps, again, this is Berkeley's failure to 'rein in yr Satyrical nature' (PC 634). After all,

---

[20] Cf. Chapter 3, section 2, pp. 36–38.

taking only twenty-one short sections to prove the mind-dependence of trees and mountains seems anything but needless prolix. But so confident is Berkeley in the truth of his central doctrine that he states that he is 'content to put the whole upon this issue':

> if you can but conceive it possible for one extended moveable substance, or in general, for any one idea or any thing like an idea, to exist otherwise than in a mind perceiving it, I shall readily give up the cause. (PHK §22)

The response to this challenge seems obvious. 'But say you, surely there is nothing easier than to imagine trees . . . in a park and nobody by to perceive them', he tells us at PHK §23. Yes, Berkeley goes on, but all one is doing is 'framing in your mind certain ideas which you call *trees* and at the same time omitting to frame the idea of anyone may perceive them'. At most, this shows that you can form ideas. It does not show that you 'can conceive it possible, that the objects of your thought may exist without the mind'. To show that 'it is necessary that you conceive them as existing unconceived or unthought of, which is a manifest repugnancy'. This sequence of thoughts (and a similar one in the *Dialogues* (DHP1 200)) is supposed to express Berkeley's 'master argument'. I said at the beginning of this chapter that there is a double irony here. First, if it *is* an argument for immaterialism, it is a poor one.[21] Secondly, I do not think Berkeley intends to offer an *argument* for immaterialism in these passages.[22] One reason to think that Berkeley *is* offering an argument for immaterialism is that he says he is 'content to put the whole on this issue'. Furthermore, he says, at PHK §23, that a 'little attention will discover to anyone the truth and evidence of what is here said, and make it unnecessary to insist on any other proofs against the existence of material substance'. That makes it sound like his key argument is given at PHK §22–3.[23]

---

[21] For an interesting take on what Berkeley says, see John Campbell, 'Berkeley's Puzzle', in T. Gendler and J. Hawthorne (eds.), *Conceivability and Possibility* (Oxford University Press, 2002), pp. 127–43.

[22] This is not an uncommon position in the literature. See, for example, Tom Stoneham, *Berkeley's World: An Examination of the Three Dialogues* (Oxford University Press, 2002), pp. 134–9.

[23] Compare DHP1 200, where Philonous says that Hylas can 'pass by all that has been hitherto said, and reckon it for nothing'.

What, then, is the argument supposed to be? It is supposed to run something like this: it is impossible to conceive an object without the mind. For any conception requires a mind to do the conceiving. When you are trying to conceive an object existing unconceived *you* are conceiving it all along! This is the contradiction to which Berkeley refers. But if this is what Berkeley is driving at, the argument is hopeless. It is, of course, impossible to be conceiving of something when one is not conceiving. But that is beside the point. Once one distinguishes between the *act* of conceiving and *what* is conceived in that act there is no problem in doing what Berkeley apparently takes to be impossible. It is not the case that you are thinking 'there is something that is at once unconceived and conceived', that would be to try to think a 'manifest repugnancy'. Instead, the content of your thought is simply the existence of a tree unconceived. It seems that Berkeley has conflated that act of conceiving with the object of conception, and so is misled into thinking that one cannot conceive something existing unconceived.[24]

There is, however, a more charitable way to see what Berkeley is driving at in these passages. It is that Berkeley is simply inviting the reader to prove that he or she can conceive the mind-independence and is then stating that they cannot. It is not an argument *for* immaterialism, but simply a way to show that one cannot prove that one can conceive what one thinks one can conceive. First, note that in PHK §22 Berkeley asks us to consider again whether one can conceive it possible for a sensible quality to exist unperceived. This 'easy trial' may make you see 'that what you contend for is a downright contradiction'. This is simply a reference back to the central argument of PHK §3.[25] The existence of an unperceived sensible object is 'perfectly unintelligible' because the being of sensible objects is to be perceived. It is *this* claim to which Berkeley refers when he says that a 'little attention will discover to any one the truth and evidence of what is here said, and make it unnecessary to insist on any other proofs against the existence of material substance'.

---

[24] Compare Pitcher, *Berkeley*, pp. 112–13. There is a complex literature that seeks to make Berkeley more sophisticated on this point, but there is a consensus that the argument ultimately fails on the grounds noted here.

[25] Compare Robert Fogelin, *Berkeley and the Principles of Human Knowledge* (London: Routledge, 2001), p. 63, and Winkler, *Berkeley: An Interpretation*, p. 187.

Secondly, since the supposition that objects exist independently of the perceiver is a 'downright contradiction', it is therefore an impossibility. We know from our discussion of abstraction that Berkeley holds that an impossibility is inconceivable. His objector thinks the supposition of things without the mind *is* conceivable. Berkeley is now challenging his imagined objector to show that this is so. The initial response is made: there is 'nothing easier than to imagine trees ... in a park, or books in a closet, and no body by to perceive them' (PHK §23). This Berkeley tells us only shows that one can frame 'in your mind certain ideas which you call *books* and *trees*, and at the same time omitting to frame the idea of anyone that may perceive them'. That is, I can visualise a tree without visualising someone looking at the tree. That act does not prove the mind-independence of the tree. What one would have to do to prove mind-independence is conceive of the tree 'existing unconceived or unthought of, which is a manifest repugnancy'. But the repugnancy to which this refers is not the one of the alleged 'master argument', but the original contradiction involved in the supposition of the existence of an unperceived sensible quality. The 'mind taking no notice of itself, is deluded to think it can and doth conceive bodies existing unthought of or without the mind'. All that remains is to explain why Berkeley talks about the existence of *unconceived* objects as a 'manifest repugnancy', rather than the repugnancy of an *unperceived* object. Granted that an unperceived object is a manifest contradiction, and so unconceivable, but here Berkeley is talking about an unconceived object. Why does that involve a manifest contradiction? The answer is that conceiving involves an object that represents the book or the tree, and that that object is itself an idea that represents by resemblance. It shares the features of the thing it represents, *including* its mind-dependence. So it would involve the attempt at conceiving of that mind-dependent object that it could exist independent of minds. You would be trying to say of an object that is mind-dependent that it is not mind-dependent, and that would be a 'manifest repugnancy'.

CHAPTER 6

Reality and God

I INTRODUCTION

The positive content of immaterialism so far offered in the *Principles* has been minimal. Sensible qualities are mind-dependent and ordinary objects are nothing but collections of sensible qualities. There are no material substances, but, Berkeley claims, there are spiritual substances. These claims raise a whole host of questions, two of which are of immediate concern. First, sensible qualities are appearances or ideas. They are 'ideas' because they are exhausted by appearance and must appear to some mind in order to exist. The 'hardness or softness, the colour, taste, warmth, figure, and suchlike qualities, which combined together constitute the several sorts of victuals and apparel, have been shewn to exist only in the mind that perceives them; and this is all that is meant by calling them *ideas*' (PHK §38). Nevertheless, when we imagine things they are appearances before the mind, and yet we do not count such appearances to the imagination (such ideas) as real things. So, if all is appearance how can we distinguish between real things and imaginary things? Secondly, can any room be found in Berkeley's system to accommodate the common-sense thought that, say, the pots and pans in my kitchen cupboard continue to exist when I am not perceiving them? On the face of it, it seems not. Sensible objects cannot exist without relation to perception and so it seems that they cannot continue to exist when unperceived. Yet we do not, for example, think that pots and pans in the cupboard cease to exist when we shut the door. So it seems, despite Berkeley's protestations to the contrary, his system offends common sense.

These two issues about real things versus imaginary things and the continuity of unperceived objects are part and parcel of the wider issue of whether Berkeley's system can provide a robust account of reality. His response and, indeed, his account of reality in general, ultimately depend on God. This, of course, raises the prior question of whether we have any reason to believe in God. In the next section of this chapter we shall sketch the argument Berkeley provides in the *Principles* of the existence of God, and his brief account of the difference between reality and imagination. Since both the argument and the account of real things offered in the *Principles* are highly compressed, it is necessary to finesse what Berkeley says here and this is something we shall do throughout this chapter, especially in sections 4 and 5 where we draw upon materials from the *Dialogues*. However, section 3 begins to address the issue of continuity as it appears in the *Principles*. Berkeley considers the objection that, contrary to what we ordinarily think, his system implies that things go out of existence when we cease to perceive them. His answer is somewhat non-committal. He allows that it is *possible* that things do continue to exist when unperceived by 'finite spirits' without committing himself that they *do* so continue. This seems a rather modest conclusion. However, it is in fact a rather difficult one to achieve, and is the subject of scholarly controversy, and I shall propose an answer, albeit a controversial one, to how continuity is possible on Berkeley's system.

With the account of how it is possible for objects to exist unperceived by you or me we then return to both the argument for the existence of God and the account of reality Berkeley offers in the context of the *Dialogues*. What is striking is that Berkeley now holds that it is not merely possible that things continue to exist unperceived by you and me, but claims that they *do* so exist. This claim feeds into what appears to be an argument for the existence of God that is different from the *Principles* one. In sections 4 and 5, I shall try to show how all the different threads come together to yield a robust account of reality. Finally, in section 6, I shall discuss some issues stemming from Berkeley's account of objects as collections of sensible qualities.

2 GOD AND REALITY: AN INITIAL ACCOUNT (PHK §§25–33)

How does Berkeley argue for God's existence in the *Principles*, and what distinction between real things and imagination does he offer? As is generally the case in the *Principles*, matters proceed swiftly. PHK §25 states that all of our 'ideas, sensations, or the things which we perceive' are causally inert. They have nothing of 'power or agency included in them'. There is nevertheless a continual change, creation and annihilation in the ideas we experience, and presumably this has some cause (PHK §26). Such a cause must be a substance, and since there are no material substances, the cause must be 'spirit', a 'simple, undivided, active being' (PHK §27). I am aware that I have direct control over some of my ideas. I can conjure up at will various ideas in my imagination when, for example, I remember Lincoln Park Zoo or imagine books in my room at home (PHK §28). However, many ideas or experiences are not similarly dependent on my will. As I look out the window all sorts of ideas come and go whether I want them to or not. Nevertheless, though not dependent on *my* spirit, they must be dependent on *some* spirit (PHK §29). Among the ideas that are not dependent on my will many exhibit a 'steadiness, order, and coherence', a certain complex ordering that appears to be rule-governed and providential in its arrangement. The 'laws of nature' – the rules under which the order of ideas fall – reveal 'the wisdom and benevolence' of the spirit that is their ground. Thus, the cause of the ideas of sense is an all powerful and benevolent creator. As Berkeley puts it much later in the *Principles*, if we:

attentively consider the constant regularity, order and concatenation of natural things, the surprising magnificence, beauty and perfection of the larger, and the exquisite contrivance of the smaller parts of creation, together with the exact harmony and correspondence of the whole ... I say if we consider all these things, and at the same time attend to the meaning and import of the attributes, one, eternal, infinitely wise, good, and perfect, we shall clearly perceive that they belong to the aforesaid spirit, *who works all in all*, and *by whom all things consist*. (PHK §146)

Hence, the ideas not caused by me and exhibiting a certain steadiness, order and coherence attest to the existence of another spirit, namely, God. What though of the distinction between imagination and real things? Well, the ideas that are 'imprinted on the senses by the Author of Nature are called *real things*: and those excited in the imagination being less regular, vivid and constant, are more properly termed *ideas*' (PHK §33). Ideas of the imagination are also less 'vivid and distinct' than real things and less 'strong, orderly and coherent'.

The sketch just offered is not significantly shorter than Berkeley's own presentation of matters in the *Principles* and leaves a tremendous amount to unpack. The first claim is that ideas are manifestly inert, so that they cannot cause change in anything, including other ideas. But is this true? Are experiences 'manifestly inert'? Berkeley invites us to introspect our experience and discover that no power or efficacy is observable. Nor are such powers hidden from us, since, being essentially appearances, experiences or ideas are completely transparent to us. There is nothing more to them than meets the eye. But it seems unclear that all experiences are passive. Think of the experience of pain. Does a painful headache not produce new thoughts or experiences? Pain can produce, for example, thoughts about how to make it stop. Berkeley must, it seems, have in mind some assumption about activity and causation that is not made explicit at PHK §25. One thought might be that he is looking for some distinct feature that can be identified as a power. The idea of pain, if it is to be active, must have some additional 'active' quality that attaches to it, but no such additional property can be detected. Alternatively, and more plausibly, Berkeley might be thinking something like the following: if *a* is the cause of *b*, then there is something in *a* that we can point to explain *why b* happened. When we understand the cause of something we just 'see' why its effect followed. But there is nothing like that in experience. What can we point to in pain that explains why it leads to 'effects' such as aversion or nausea? To say 'because it hurts' seems to say nothing more than to say that the 'cause' is a pain, and not what it is about the pain that explains its effect. Pain might typically be *followed* by aversion or nausea, but there is nothing in the pain that explains why.

Suppose that this is correct and that ideas are passive. Why then does Berkeley think that spiritual substances are *active*?[1] The claim seems to rest on the intuition that ideas are subject to my will. I can summon at will ideas of red, of unicorns or whatever else it is possible for me to imagine. I can also choose not to have those ideas (I can by *fiat* cease to imagine a unicorn). Of course, some ideas come to mind unbidden. The idea of that steak one plans to have for dinner can

---

[1] There is actually a prior question of why Berkeley is confident that there are spirits at all, and we shall pursue this in Chapter 8, section 3.

suddenly pop into one's mind. But such ideas are still under one's volitional control inasmuch as one can decide to think of something else. 'This making and unmaking ideas doth very properly denominate the mind active', Berkeley tells us at PHK §28, that is, our notion of power comes from the awareness of our will.[2] But how does the will furnish any conception of power?[3] Again, Berkeley is not explicit. It might be that he takes it to be evident to introspection. It is, as philosophers would say, a phenomenological datum. But there might also be another thought at play here. Something is a cause if, and only if, it can answer the question of just why such and such (the effect) happens. When a person (spirit) does something we can always ask for a *reason* why they did such and such. If I went to the Cubs game at Wrigley Field, someone can ask why I did so, and I can reply that it was because I enjoy baseball. The connection between my will and what follows it is not simply that B follows A, but B is *intelligible* or *makes sense* in light of A. My going to the baseball (an effect) happened *because* I enjoy baseball.

Let us grant Berkeley the claim that ideas are passive and spirits are active.[4] Ideas 'actually perceived by sense' are not under the direct control of my will, and must, therefore, be caused by some other spirit. Such ideas are 'strong and lively, and distinct', and fall into patterns of 'steadiness, order and coherence'. But what does Berkeley mean when he says that the ideas of sense are more 'vivid', 'lively', 'strong' and 'distinct'? And what are 'steadiness, order and coherence'? Let us begin with the first notions, and try to illustrate them with an example. Look at the page you are presently reading. Now, close your eyes and form a mental picture of the page. The mental picture will be much fainter – less 'strong and lively' – than the experience you have of the page when you are looking at it. The mental image is very likely

---

[2] Recall from Chapter 2, section 6, p. 29 that Locke held that we gain whatever understanding of power we have from an awareness of the activity of our wills. This obscure understanding of power is what allows us to attribute it to material substance, albeit in a way that yields no understanding of such powers.

[3] Louis Loeb points out that these sections of the PHK do not really contain an argument for the claim that all power is volitional (*From Descartes to Hume: Continental Metaphysics and the Development of Modern Philosophy* (Ithaca: Cornell University Press, 1981), pp. 263–8). Nevertheless, I think this assumption is in play, since Berkeley presents such an argument elsewhere (see DHP3 239). I owe this point to the unpublished work of Tom Curtin.

[4] We shall see in Chapter 8 that Berkeley has serious problems here.

not to have the detail and clarity of the visual experience – it is not as 'distinct'. These features are features of *particular* experiences. The second set of criteria applies to *sequences* of experiences. The visual experiences I have as I look out of the window follow a sequence that that has a steadiness, order and coherence that mere imagination lacks. We think that things fall into regular patterns (fire tends to burn things, the sun casts shadows) in an order where one thing follows another. We can also give coherent accounts of the changes in the sequences of experiences, even when our perception of that sequence is interrupted. To borrow an example from Hume, the fire in the hearth was burning brightly when I left my study, but when I returned all that remained was its dim embers. From this we are also supposed to think that this order exhibits something that entitles us to believe that the arrangement is providential in character, that it exhibits some 'wise contrivance' that contributes to the wellbeing of finite spirits.

I will leave the reader to decide how plausible this is, but Berkeley holds that we recognise that experience has all these features and that the best explanation of these features is the causal activity of the infinite spirit. Berkeley's argument is usually held to be a version of the argument from design.[5] The argument takes the complexity and ordering in the universe to be evidence of a designing intelligence. This is an argument that came under considerable fire in the eighteenth century from Hume's 1776 *Dialogues Concerning Natural Religion*. Why must the complexity be the work of a single mind? How does the course of experience suggest a wholly benevolent mind when there is much pain and misery? Why does complexity and order require an intelligent designing cause? After all, a chicken produces an egg, but the chicken can hardly be said to have designed it. Berkeley is vulnerable to much of Hume's criticism, but it is worth noting that Berkeley's argument has a feature that distinguishes it from other versions: Berkeley's view that all causation involves the will implies that if there is a cause of order in the universe then it is a mind. Other versions allow that there are causes other than minds, but order suggests that the cause of order is most probably a mind. Berkeley's

---

[5] Robert Fogelin suggests that Berkeley in some passages is trying to show that knowledge of God is intuitive. See his *Berkeley and the* Principles of Human Knowledge, pp. 72–4.

view that only minds are causes means that the cause of the universe must be a mind.

I do not propose to say more in assessing this argument. Let me instead briefly comment on Berkeley's *Principles'* account of in what reality consists. The ideas of the imagination differ from the ideas of sense (real things) in that the latter are more lively or vivid than the former. But this admits of two readings. Is their being more lively or vivid than other ideas that constitute their reality or is what *constitutes* their reality the fact that they are caused by God and their strength and liveliness is merely *evidence* of this? If it is the former, the account is implausible. It seems perfectly possible for one's imagination to be far more vivid and striking than one's sense perception. Someone sat in a darkened silent room might take some hallucinogenic drugs and enjoy a host of experiences more lively and vivid than those delivered by his senses. Now it might be replied that Berkeley also includes orderliness and coherence in his account of reality, but again one can begin to think of cases where hallucinations are orderly and coherent (think of a clever scientist who learns to manipulate your brain). What looks more plausible is that real things are the class of ideas caused by God and the strength, order and coherence of such ideas is a reliable *sign* that they are so caused.[6] Real things are those ideas caused by God and typically these are steady and coherent, etc.

It is not clear from the *Principles* which interpretation is Berkeley's. Even when he sounds most committed to the idea that strength, orderliness and coherence are constitutive of reality, things are far from straightforward. Ideas of sense:

are said to have more reality [than those of the mind perceiving them]: by which meant that they are affecting, orderly, and distinct; and that they are not fictions of the imagination. (PHK §36)

The first half of this passage suggests that real things consist in the fact that they are 'affecting, orderly, and distinct', but the second suggests something different, namely, that they are 'not fictions of the mind'. Berkeley cannot simply mean by 'not fictions of the mind' that they are real things, since that is precisely what is trying to be understood. Rather, it must mean that such ideas are not *created* by me nor are they

⁶ Compare Fogelin, *Berkeley and the* Principles of Human Knowledge, p. 69.

inventions of mine, but instead are created by God and it is this that constitutes their reality.

As I mentioned, the *Principles* argument for the existence of God and Berkeley's account of the nature of real things is extremely compressed. We shall return to aspects of it – and in particular the sense in which God is the cause of the ideas of sense and how this is related to the category of real things– in order to refine these notions. Let us now turn to what Berkeley has to say about the continuity of objects in the *Principles*. This will help us to understand the nature of God's causation of the ideas of sense and the nature of real things.

3 GOD, MIND-DEPENDENCE AND THE POSSIBILITY OF CONTINUOUS EXISTENCE

From PHK §34 to §84 Berkeley considers a range of objections to his system. A key objection is raised at PHK §45, which asks whether, if objects are perception-dependent, they thereby cease to exist when not perceived. Is it not the case that 'things are every moment annihilated and created anew' as they are at one time perceived and another time unperceived? After reminding the reader that unperceived existence is inconceivable, and pointing to some further problems with the materialist position (PHK §§46–7), Berkeley answers the objection in the following way. Although the being of sensible objects is to be perceived:

we may not hence conclude they have no existence except only when perceived by us, since there may be some other spirit that perceives them, though we do not. Wherever bodies are said to have no existence without the mind, I would not be understood to mean this or that particular mind, but all minds whatsoever. It does not therefore follow from the foregoing principles, that bodies are annihilated and created every moment, or exist not at all during the intervals between our perception of them. (PHK §48)

The natural way to take this is that it is possible for objects (collections of sensible qualities) to exist when not perceived by us (finite creatures) in virtue of their being perceived by some other spirit. That spirit would be God, if we pick up on what Berkeley says earlier, namely, that when things are not perceived by us they 'either have no existence at all, or else subsist in the mind of some eternal spirit' (PHK

§6). Now, as I mentioned, Berkeley does not commit himself to saying that objects *do* continue to exist when unperceived by us. The texts simply suggest that it is possible that they so exist because it may be the case that God perceives them. That sounds straightforward, but even granting that possibility is more complicated than it may seem.

The view that God could maintain the continuous existence of objects unperceived by us by perceiving them is, unsurprisingly, known as the 'perception theory'.[7] However, the claim that God perceives objects appears immediately to fall foul of the fact that Berkeley explicitly denies that God can perceive anything by sense. 'God knows or hath ideas; but His ideas are not convey'd to Him by sense, as ours are' (DHP3 241). This can suggest that all his ideas are intellectual and so his ideas cannot be sensible qualities. Rather than perceiving sensible qualities as we do he perceives them in the sense that he knows or comprehends them.[8] Furthermore, if sensible objects are composites of qualities that are *caused in us* by God, then it seems odd to say that they continue to exist, though, at the same time that they are not caused in us (we are, after all, not perceiving the sensible objects).

We shall return to the perception theory below, but if it is rejected, what should we put in its place? One option is to read Berkeley as being, shall we say, a little elastic about the sense in which the objects we perceive might continue to exist in the mind of God. What he must really mean is not that the sensible objects we sometimes perceive continue to exist when we do not perceive them, but rather that God has intellectual ideas *of* the sensible objects he causes in the minds of finite spirits and so in this, extended, sense objects continue to exist unperceived. He conceives of them rather than perceives them (by sense) and, hence, this position is termed the 'conception theory'. This is perhaps why he chooses to say such objects 'subsist in the mind of some eternal spirit' (PHK §6), rather than 'exist'. But the elasticity here is at full stretch and the conception theory is strained. First, it is not true that the objects we perceive continue to exist when not perceived. God's intellect ideas are not the same things as sensible objects. Secondly, the theory seems to collapse the distinction between actual and possible objects. God can conceive (have ideas

---

[7] After Pitcher, *Berkeley*, p. 175.   [8] Compare Pitcher, *Berkeley*, p. 175.

of) not merely of what things there are, but what there could be (unicorns, for example). Does that mean that all possible objects, as well as actual objects, 'subsist' in the mind of God, and, if so, does that mean that there really is no distinction between actual and possible objects?

Both the perception and conception theories are versions of *idealism*. Objects are collections of actual ideas. A third view on unperceived existence is phenomenalism, which was mentioned in the last chapter.[9] It differs from idealism because it holds that objects are collections not merely of actual ideas, but collections of actual and *possible* ideas. Since an object consists not merely in actual ideas, but also possible ideas, an object continues to exist unperceived by us in virtue of the fact that it is true that were we in such and such circumstances we would have such and such ideas. To put it another way, an object continues to exist in that there is a set of truths regarding which ideas I would perceive under such and such circumstances, and this set constitutes what is meant by the relevant sensible object. Thus, at PHK §3, Berkeley writes that the table 'exists, that is, I see and feel it; and if I were out of my study I should say it existed, meaning thereby if I was in my study I might perceive it'.

How does God fit into this picture? Well, if we claim that what I mean by such and such an object is not merely the actual ideas I have, but what ideas I would have under different circumstances, then the question arises of what it is that makes it true that I would have such and such ideas were I under such and such a circumstance. What makes it true that were I to look in my kitchen cupboard I would have pots and pans related ideas? The answer is that all the relevant truths are true in virtue of the fact that God's will is structured systematically such that he will cause such and such ideas under those circumstances. There are 'powers' to produce such and such ideas that are grounded in 'the active Being' (PC 52). Phenomenalism has a neat way of avoiding one objection levelled at the Conception Theory, namely, that it collapses the distinction between actual and possible objects. God has ideas of unicorns and so unicorns are possible objects, but they are not actual objects because God has chosen not to cause in us

[9] The best defence of a phenomenalist reading of Berkeley is Winkler's *Berkeley: An Interpretation*, ch. 7.

the relevant sensible objects under any circumstances. God also has ideas of actual objects, and what makes them actual is that he also wills to produce in us the corresponding sensible ideas.

There are texts where Berkeley seems to flirt with phenomenalism, including the one quoted above.[10] Nevertheless, there is an exchange in the *Dialogues* that makes it very difficult to read Berkeley as a phenomenalist. Phenomenalism is equivalent to the claim that an object exists in virtue of its being perceivable rather than its being actually perceived. Hylas suggests this position to Philonous by saying, 'I grant the existence of a sensible thing consists in being perceivable, but not in being actually perceived' (DHP3 234). This gives Philonous the opportunity to voice a phenomenalist position on the existence of objects by saying something like, 'Yes, the yonder tree exists because it is perceivable, meaning were I to open my eyes I may receive several ideas.' But he does not do so. Instead, he asks 'And what is perceivable but an idea? And how can an idea exist without actually being perceived?' Here he is tying existence not with being perceivable, but with actually being perceived.

So how then are we to understand the possibility that the pots and pans in my cupboard continue to exist unperceived by us? I think the objections to the perception theory are not as strong as many hold, and, in fact, it offers the best account of Berkeley's position. The main objection is that God cannot perceive anything by sense. But it is, I think, an objection that can be met. The fact that God cannot perceive *by sense* does not entail that he cannot perceive sensible qualities. It is these objects we perceive and he perceives them as well. When Berkeley asserts that God does not perceive anything by sense, the emphasis is not on *what* is perceived (sensible qualities), but on *how* it is perceived. Why God does not perceive by sense is because to perceive by sense requires the perceiver to be passive. It involves the perceiver be affected by an external agent and that cannot be true of God:

God, whom no external being can affect, who perceives nothing by sense as we do, whose will is absolute and independent, causing all things, and liable to be thwarted by nothing; it is evident, such a being as this can suffer

---

[10] See also PHK §58 and PC 52, 98, 282 and 293a.

nothing, nor be affected with any painful sensation or indeed any sensation at all. (DHP3 241)

This leaves open the possibility that God perceives sensible qualities, but not because those sensible qualities are 'impressed upon him' by some external agent. His perception of such qualities must therefore involve his being wholly active, and such perception must therefore consist in his *creating* or *bringing* into being sensible objects.[11] The difference between us and God on this score is that our powers of creative perception are limited to bringing into being the ideas of the imagination (it is here we are active in the creation of ideas, but passive with respect to the ideas that constitute the real world). God is active through and through.

It might be objected that the texts suggest something other than that God cannot perceive by sense because that would make him passive. Instead, the point is that God cannot have *sensations*. That concerns not *how* he perceives, but *what* is perceived. Now, *if* the mind-dependence on the sensible were as the IS interpretation would have it, then sensible qualities are just collections of 'private' sensations, and it would seem problematic to read God as a perceiver of them. But there are two things to be said about what it said in the text above about the relation between God and sensation. The first thing that Berkeley is asking is whether God can be *affected by* sensation, and God's not being affected by sensations is consistent with his having them. His particular example is pain, where two senses of 'suffer' are in play. One is the sense in which sense perception is passive. The second is the moral sense in which one suffers, namely, due to the sheer unpleasantness of pain. None of this entails that God does not have awareness of the essentially qualitative character associated with pain, or redness, or any other sensible quality. As Philonous says, God 'knows . . . among other things what pain is, even every sort of painful sensation' (DHP3 241). Secondly, on the EP inter-pretation of mind-dependence, the mind-dependence of the sensible is not understood as the assimilation of sensible qualities to sensations. Instead, the claim is that we cannot understand any sensible quality except in terms of its being essentially an appearance for some mind. As we noted in the previous chapter, this notion of mind-dependence does

---

[11] See Melissa Frankel, 'Berkeley and God in the Quad', *Philosophy Compass* 7 (2012), 338–96, to whom I owe this suggestion.

not tie the existence of a sensible quality to any *particular* mind, but rather that its existence must consist in appearing to some mind. The pots and pans consist in a collection of appearances, and though they are not appearances *for me* when they are in the cupboard, they continue to exist because they appear to the infinite spirit.

This fits neatly with the fact that in PHK §48 Berkeley stresses that when he is talking about the dependence of the sensible on minds he does not mean 'this or that particular mind'. If sensible objects were just collections of sensations, then their existence would be dependent on this or that particular mind. The only sense in which they would not depend on my mind would consist in the fact that it is God who causes those sensations in me. But we should resist this model of God's activity. God's causal activity should not be understood as causing distinct sets of private sensations in different minds. Instead, his active perception consists in the creation of objects – sets of sensible qualities – that exist independently of any finite minds. On the former view the real world would consist simply in the simultaneous and coordinated production of private sensation. It is as if God kicks us all on the shin at the same time so we all experience sensations as the same time. Instead, tables and chairs, though composed of qualities that are essentially appearances, are there independently of your or my experience of them. It is God who creates those sensible qualities through his active perception, but their existence does not consist in a matter of our having private sensations the sequences of which are coordinated by God. Tables, chairs and real things are independent of your or my subjective states and acts of perception.

Real things are therefore independent of you and me. They are brought into existence by God's perception of them, not yours or mine. There are a number of qualifications to add to this claim, but let us first turn to the *Dialogues* and try to see why Berkeley moves from holding that it is merely possible that objects continue to exist when not perceived by us to holding that they in fact do, and how this informs his case for the existence of God.

4 THE *DIALOGUES* ARGUMENT, INDEPENDENCE AND CONTINUITY

At the beginning of this chapter I mentioned that it is common to suppose that Berkeley presents an argument for the existence of God in the *Dialogues* which is different from the argument of the *Principles*. The latter is customarily referred to as the 'passivity argument' and the *Dialogues* argument as the 'continuity argument'.[12] The *Principles* argument moves from the fact that I am passive with respect to some ideas to the conclusion that there must be another spirit who causes them (hence 'passivity'). The *Dialogues* argument, by contrast, appears to move from the fact that since ideas are independent of my mind they must *exist in* another mind. Because they so exist they *continue* to exist in that mind. The argument begins from the immaterialist thesis that 'sensible things cannot exist otherwise than in a mind or spirit', but, Philonous continues,

> I conclude [from this], not that they have no real existence, but that seeing that they depend not on my thought, and have an existence distinct from being perceived by me, *there must be some other mind wherein they exist*. As sure therefore as the sensible world really exists, so sure is there an infinite omnipresent spirit who contains and supports it. (DHP2 212)

A similar claim is made at DHP3 230. Hylas asks Philonous whether he can conceive 'it possible that things perceivable by sense may still exist' when not perceived by him, and Philonous replies:

> I can; but then it must be in another mind. When I deny sensible things an existence out of the mind, I do not mean my mind in particular, but all minds. Now it is plain they have an existence exterior to my mind, since I find them by experience to be independent of it. There is therefore some other mind wherein they exist, during the intervals between the times of my perceiving them.

Some see Berkeley's continuity argument as showing that he has muddled up two senses of independence. It is one thing to say that, say, the pain in my shin is causally independent of me (it was caused by you kicking me), and quite another to say that it is ontologically independent of me, namely, that exists independently of me. Berkeley is moving illegitimately from the claim that sensible objects are not *caused* by me to the conclusion that they must be *perceived* by some other spirit. He must be muddling the notion of independence as 'not caused by me' – the notion of independence at play in the passivity

---

[12] The terms originate from Jonathan Bennett. See his *Locke, Berkeley, Hume: Central Themes* (Oxford University Press, 1971), pp. 165–85.

argument – with a different one, namely, 'not existing in me' or not 'owned by me'.[13] It is like thinking that, when you kick me in the shin, because you are the cause of that pain you must also perceive that pain.

Looked at this way, Berkeley makes a mistake in the *Dialogues* that he avoided in the *Principles*. But perhaps, instead, he came to realise in the *Dialogues* that his commitments offered him more resources than he previously thought. Crucial to the *Dialogues* is the notion of the *independence* of ideas from finite spirits. If we understand the mind-*dependence* of sensible objects along the IS interpretation, then the only sense in which sensible objects can be understood as independent of me is akin to the example above, of you kicking me in the shin. Sensible objects would by this view be ontologically dependent of my particular mind (they depend on my mind for their existence), but causally independent since it is some other spirit that brings about that existence in my mind. So it would be a very bad mistake to move from causal independence to a claim that some other mind perceives sensible qualities. But the notion of independence from finite minds allowed by the EP interpretation is more robust than this. Sensible qualities depend on some perceiver for their existence, but not on any particular mind. They are not like sensations, which can exist only in the particular minds that experience them. Sensible qualities are ontologically independent of finite minds, though not ontologically independent of all spirits. Since, therefore, we can tell that sensible qualities are independent of finite minds, but require some perceiver for their existence, I can conclude that their existence depends on another perceiver, for the very model of the causation of sensible qualities or ideas is God's active perception of those qualities. So not being brought into existence by me – the ontological independence of sensible qualities – requires some spirit whose perception causes them or, in other words, brings them into existence. I can tell that they have this independent existence, because I can tell that their existence is not down to my will. So, the existence of sensible qualities, and the objects that are compositions of them, must be brought about by the activity of another spirit, an activity that consists in the 'making and unmaking ideas [which] doth very properly denominate the mind active'

---

[13] See Bennett, *Locke, Berkeley, Hume*, pp. 170–2.

(PHK §28). The existence of the sensible world is dependent upon God's active perception, and I can be confident that it continues to exist when unperceived by finite minds.

What changes in the *Dialogues* is that Berkeley realises that the causal independence of the ideas of sense does not merely show that they are caused by an infinite spirit, but also involves *bringing them into existence* by perceiving them (since their dependence is not a matter of dependence on particular finite minds). So God's causal activity consists in his perceiving sensible qualities, an activity that is matched by our passivity in our perception. So rather than seeing Berkeley as offering two different arguments (the 'passivity argument' and a different 'continuity argument'), I think it is better to think of them as two versions of an 'independence argument'. In the *Principles*, Berkeley focuses on the notion of independence as causal independence: sensible qualities are not caused by the activity of my will. In the *Dialogues*, the ontological independence of sensible qualities comes to the fore, whereby the ontological independence of sensible qualities from me, together with immaterialism's central thesis that sensible qualities are perception-dependent, implies their ontological dependency on the mind of God.

5 REALITY, EXHIBITION AND CREATION

If sensible objects are independent of finite perceivers and exist in virtue of God's active perception, what are we to make of the account of the distinction between real and imaginary things sketched above in section 2? The ideas associated with 'real things' are so marked by being 'more affecting, orderly and distinct' (PHK §36) than ideas of the imagination. I suggested that these features are best thought of as indicative of their reality, rather than constitutive of it. What constitutes the difference between real things and the ideas of the imagination is that the existence of the former is caused by God and the latter caused by us. Now we can afford to be a little more precise about the expression 'caused by God'. What this does *not* mean is what the IS reading would suggest, namely, that God causes in individual minds a set of private sensations, so that your kicking me in the shin brings about pain in me. It is, rather, that the universe of sensible objects is brought into existence by God's active perception, and it is these objects that constitute a reality that is independent of finite minds. No doubt the fact that Berkeley talks about sensible objects as collections of ideas encourages a view that God is causing subjective states 'in' the mind of individuals, but as we have already seen Berkeley discourages that view of ideas.[14] The notion that sensible qualities are ideas is explained by the EP interpretation of their mind-dependence.

Nevertheless, simply stating that real things are those sensible qualities brought into existence by God's perception does not get to the heart of things, for two reasons. The first concerns that fact that Berkeley talks of real things 'being imprinted on the senses' (PHK §33). That, again, might encourage the IP reading's view that this consists in our having subjective states caused 'in' us by God. But this is not the only way to read this expression. It is, rather, that the object must be *exhibited* or *presented to* the mind in order for it to be perceived by a finite mind. To perceive by sense is to be passive, and ideas are themselves passive. The event of perceiving requires something active, and here God is active not merely in his perception of sensible objects, but also in revealing or presenting those objects to the mind.

This requirement on real things – that not only are they actively perceived by God, but are also exhibited to finite creatures – also helps us to understand Berkeley's response to a worry about how immaterialism can be consistent with the traditional mosaic account of God's creation of the world. This brings us to the second complication in simply identifying real things with those whose existence is sustained by the active perception of God. It will take a little while to see quite what the issue is, however, so let us begin by looking at why the traditional account of creation is a matter of concern for Berkeley.

God created human beings on the sixth day, but created other things before he created human beings. But if things depend on perceivers for their existence, how could such things, such as the sun, the moon and stars, exist when they were supposedly created on the fourth day? Hylas presents this as a problem and Philonous says in reply:

When things are said to begin or end their existence, we do not mean this with regard to God, but his creatures . . . when things before imperceptible to

----

[14] See Chapter 4, section 4, pp. 62–69.

creatures, are by a decree of God, made perceptible to them; then are they said to have a relative existence, with respect to created minds. (DHP3 251–2)

Hylas objects that this says nothing to the point. A 'relative' or 'hypothetical' existence is not an 'absolute' existence. After suggesting that non-human creatures might have perceived them prior to the creation of humanity, Philonous repeats the immaterialist claim that the 'absolute' existence of sensible qualities is empty.

Hylas changes tack at this stage and argues that since all things are eternally known by God and 'the existence of sensible things consist in their being in a mind', there cannot be any beginning to the existence of sensible things. Again, Philonous repeats that prior to the creation of human beings the world has 'a relative, or hypothetical existence' that consists in the fact that God decrees that sensible objects become perceptible even though not yet perceived. This allows a 'twofold state of things, the one ectypal or natural, the other archetypal and eternal' (DHP3 254).

What are we to make of this exchange? Some commentators detect a hint of phenomenalism, where creation is the creation of the possibilities of perception – possible ideas – even though such objects are not actually perceived.[15] Philonous' statement of a 'hypothetical' or 'relative' existence, an allusion to a phenomenalist position, and the problem to which the exchange is alluding is the alleged fact that things exist only when perceived by human creatures because God is not perceiver. However, I do not think this is what Philonous is driving at here. One problem which this exchange brings out is a problem about simply identifying real things with those things which God brings into existence by active perception. God's perception of things (which we have thus far said are real things) is eternal. That is a consequence of a certain theological thesis about the unchangeable nature of God. But if *real* things exist eternally in the mind of God, how on earth could they be *created*? Either reality has to have a moment of creation, as the mosaic account suggests, or it exists eternally in the activity perception of God. What we need now to be able to distinguish is the *actual*, the *possible* and the *real*. We noted above that we can distinguish in the mind of God actual from possible things by taking the former to be

[15] See, e.g., Winkler, *Berkeley: An Interpretation*, pp. 220–2.

actual in virtue of God perceiving them, and the merely possible in terms simply of his having intellectual ideas. Now, the real must be distinguished from the actual because the when 'things are said to begin or end their existence, we do not mean this with regard to God, but his creatures' (DHP3 251–2). So Berkeley must distinguish the actual from the real by appealing to the idea that actual things become real things (are properly thought of as created) when God renders them *perceptible* to us. Actual things become *real* things by God's decree that they become perceivable. Thus, in a letter to Lady Percival (who originally raised the issue) Berkeley writes:

I do not deny the existence of any of those sensible qualities which Moses says were created by God. They existed from all eternity in the Divine intellect, and then became perceptible (i.e., were created) in the same manner and order as described in Genesis.[16]

Actual things become real things (are created) by becoming perceptible. That is something he can do on the days before the creation of human beings, and so the sun, the moon and the stars were created in this sense before us. But the difference between the actual and the real does not conflict with the perception theory of continuity. For the things we perceive in virtue of God's activity of exhibiting them to us (causing to perceive them) are identical to the actual things whose existence depends on God's active perception.

6 PHYSICAL OBJECTS: IDENTITY, PERCEPTION AND OBJECTIVITY

Having given some account of both the continuity and reality of physical objects, let us now turn to examine some further issues concerning physical objects. Some of them turn on Berkeley's rejection of substance, and his claim that ordinary objects like trees and tables are nothing but collections of sensible qualities. Others concern our perception of such objects.

In exploring this issue of continuity we have been talking about sensible or physical *objects*. But from God's perspective the actual is

---

[16] Berkeley to Percival, 6 September 1710, in Luce and Jessop (eds), *The Works of George Berkeley*, vol. 8, p. 37.

identical to the sum total of sensible qualities. It is we time-bound creatures with practical concerns who group these different sensory qualities into objects like chairs, trees or tables. As we noted, Berkeley holds that how we 'carve up' the vast array of sensible qualities into the objects of common sense is a matter of convention (see Chapter 4, section 2). We might sometimes suppose that there is 'one single, unchanged, unperceivable, real nature, marked by each name [like apple or tree]', but this is a mistake, one encouraged by a casual interpretation of language when we come to speak 'of several distinct ideas, as united into one thing in the mind'. The names for objects, however, reflect groupings that are 'merely for conveniency and dispatch in the common actions of life, without any regard to speculation' (DHP3 245–6). This not to say that sensible qualities are not connected in any way. There are complex sets of *semantic* relations between sensible qualities, which we shall discuss in the next chapter. In exploring these connections, Philonous tells us, the 'more one is said to know of the nature of things' (DHP3 245). But our ordinary catalogue of objects is a human invention.[17]

This view of physical objects invites a large number of issues. One issue, or rather related set of issues, turns on identity. The reason the notion of substance appeals to some philosophers is precisely because of identity. We naturally talk of the qualities *of* objects, and this suggests the notion of a thing distinct from the qualities that possess those qualities. Positing a substance secures, in other words, what is known as the *synchronic* identity of a thing. It accounts for how the properties of a thing are related at any one time. Berkeley allows that the *word* 'substance' is perfectly fine as long as it is used in what he claims to be its 'vulgar sense', namely, a combination of sensible qualities (PHK §37), but he rejects the problematic notion of substance as a thing distinct from these qualities that is their 'owner'. When we say the die is hard or cuboid we are not, suggests Berkeley, attributing a quality to something distinct from the collection of qualities, but instead expressing what is part of the meaning of the term 'die' (PHK §49). This, however, invites a question that Berkeley

---

[17] For interesting challenges to this standard view, see Richard Glauser, 'The Problem of the Unity of a Physical Object in Berkeley', in S. Daniel (ed.), *Reexamining Berkeley's Philosophy* (University of Toronto Press, 2007), pp. 50–81.

does not address. Not every quality possessed by an object need be constitutive of what that object is. What it is to be a die is to have a particular shape, but, though a die must have some colour, there is no particular colour it must be in order to count as a die. It can be red, white or black and still be a die. An account of how to divide those qualities that are 'part of the meaning' of an object, and those which are not, is therefore required.

The success or otherwise of this project is related to another issue in identity. Berkeley distinguishes between a vulgar and an abstracted philosophical sense of identity (which, of course, he rejects). Philonous tells Hylas the following:

suppose a house, whose walls or outward shell remaining unaltered, the chambers are all pulled down, and new ones built in their place; and that you should call this the *same*, and I should say it was not the *same* house: would we not for all this perfectly agree in our thoughts of the house, considered in itself? If you should say, we differed in our notions; for that you superadded to your idea of the house the simple abstracted idea of identity, whereas I did not; I would tell you I know not what you mean by that *abstracted idea of identity*. (DHP3 248)

This passage concerns the conditions of identity through change. What is it that makes x numerically the same as y even though there has been a change of properties (the house has had its rooms replaced but we nevertheless think it is the very same house). Since change of properties is bound up with time, the identity issue here is often referred to as one of *diachronic* identity. Before we briefly discuss what Berkeley has to say (or rather does not say) about this topic, the passage above suggests something that is fundamental to the question of identity. Whether x and y are numerically identical depends on just what *sort* of object we are considering. As such, the descriptions associated with determining kinds of things build into themselves criteria of identity, and there is no sense attached to the question whether x and y are the same thing that can be abstracted from those particular descriptions. If we agree as to the meaning of 'house' (or 'perfectly agree in our thoughts of the house'), then there is no further issue about the criteria of identity for that thing.

What, then, of the diachronic identity of objects? We may think that objects maintain their identity through changes in their qualities or properties. If particular things are substances, then we can think simply in terms of a change in that substance's properties. But what can we say about the identity of some particular object through change when it is just a collection of properties?[18] To illustrate the worry, recall the Descartes' piece of wax which we discussed in Chapter 2, section 3. At room temperature, it has a white colour, a certain texture, shape and smell. If, however, we apply heat to the wax all those sensible qualities are replaced by different ones. Whiteness is replaced by translucency, its square shape is replaced by a puddle, its original smell by another. For Descartes, this example is part of his case for the existence of a substance that underlies such change. He thinks that we still recognise that it is the same piece of wax despite these changes, and this suggests that there is some underlying substance. Berkeley will reject that claim, of course, but what can he say to accommodate the intuition that it is the same piece of wax? The most promising line he could take is as follows. What makes any thing the thing it is are the sensible qualities that compose it, but this should not be confused with the sum of sensible qualities at *any one particular time*. Instead, the wax comprises a set of sensible qualities that stretches through time from its beginning to its end. The sensible qualities associated with the wax before the event of melting constitute a *part* of the wax, those after the melting are a different part of the wax. These parts are called 'temporal' parts. So the same object persists through change because the different qualities belong to different temporal parts of the wax.

The issues we have just briefly touched upon did not much concern Berkeley.[19] I suspect this is because he thought that since human interests determine our grouping of sensible qualities into objects, fine questions about the identity criteria were of little importance to him (see DHP3 247). Two further issues concern our *perception* of such objects. Both of these relate to our common-sense conception of the

---

[18] Berkeley was aware of this worry. Thus, in the notebooks he writes: 'On account of my doctrine the identity of finite substances must consist in something else than continued existence ... the existence of our thoughts (wch being combin'd make all substances) being frequently interrupted, & having divers beginnings, & endings' (PC 194). Note that this is not a denial that sensible qualities continue to exist independently of finite spirits, only that our mind-dependent grouping changes.

[19] For more extensive discussion, see Stoneham, *Berkeley's World*, ch. 8.

world and our relation to it. The first, which we left hanging from Chapter 4, section 2, concerns whether we immediately perceive sensible objects or merely sensible qualities. If Berkeley really holds that we only perceive qualities rather than objects, this appears to leave him in an uncomfortable position, since common sense has it that we perceive things or objects rather than just qualities. The second issue concerns what is called 'interpersonal perception'. We think that numerically the same object can be perceived by two or more persons. You and I can see the very same cup. The issue is just how is this possible in Berkeley's system.

Let us begin with the first issue. One reason offered to show that we only immediately perceive qualities came from the *Dialogues* discussion concerning the hearing of the noise of a coach (mentioned in Chapter 4, section 2). Philonous tells us that in 'truth and strictness, nothing can be *heard* but *sound*; and the coach is not then properly perceived by sense, but suggested from experience' (DHP1 204). Does this really mean that Berkeley must hold that we cannot immediately perceive objects? To see why not, we must begin by examining what lies behind Philonous' claim. What the claim expresses is Berkeley's 'heterogeneity thesis'. Qualities perceived by different senses are of entirely distinct kinds, and no quality is perceived by more than one sense; by sight we perceive only colour and visible extension and by touch only tangible extension (see, for example, PHK §44). Visible and tangible extension are distinct kinds of property and are never perceived by any sense other than their proper sense. Berkeley's writings on vision make extensive use of this heterogeneity thesis, dividing qualities into different kinds he terms the 'proper' immediate objects of the respective senses. So perhaps what Berkeley is telling us with the coach example is that the coach is not *properly* perceived because the different senses have different qualities as their proper objects. This might allow for a sense of immediate perception, though improper, that would allow that the object – the coach – is immediately perceived.[20]

How? An object is a collection of qualities, but, of course, for a whole host of reasons, not all the qualities that constitute that object

---

[20] Compare George Pappas, *Berkeley's Thought* (Ithaca: Cornell University Press, 2000), pp. 178 ff.

are perceived at once. We do not, for example, see the back of a chair when looking at the front. Furthermore, since the object is the sum of sensible qualities across time (as noted in the discussion of diachronic identity above) only a temporal *part* of an object is present at a given time, rather than the whole object. It is independently plausible, nevertheless, to suppose that we can and do perceive an object when perceiving a *part* of that object. Suppose I open the drawer of my study desk and see the edge of my phone poking up through various bits of clutter. Its seems perfectly natural to say that I see my phone, even though I do not see *all* of my phone. On Berkeley's view of things the phone is just a collection of sensible qualities, and when I look in my drawer I immediately perceive a few of those qualities that enter into its composition. Nevertheless, I am immediately perceiving the phone because I am immediately perceiving a part of it, that is, a subset of the sensible qualities that enter into its composition.

In allowing that we perceive an object (the entire collection of sensible qualities) by seeing only some of its members, it is important to note that this is not equivalent to *knowing* or even *believing* that we are perceiving the object of which that set of sensible qualities is a part. Suppose I have a different electronic device, a guitar tuner, say, that looks just the same as my phone when placed at a similar angle amid the clutter in my desk drawer. I know that the guitar tuner is in my drawer as well as my phone, and knowing that might make me wonder whether I know it is my phone that I am seeing. So I might, therefore, confine myself to a weaker claim about what I can *know* to be immediately perceiving, namely, a certain black shape. For all I know this might be the guitar tuner. But it does not follow from this that it is not the phone that I am perceiving. It is, rather, that I have a reason not to form the judgement *that* it is my phone. At play here is a distinction between judgemental and non-judgemental perceiving. One can see something without knowing or judging that what one sees is an *x* or a *y*. You, for example, might go through the drawers in my desk and see the guitar tuner, but because you have no knowledge of guitar tuners you will not see *that* there is a guitar tuner – you would describe it as a black box with some lights on it. Seeing or recognising *that* it is a guitar tuner is the judgemental sense of perceiving.

The immediate perception of a sensible object through the immediate perception of a part of that object is centrally a case of non-judgemental perception. This is important to note, because it might be thought that since Philonous tells us that the coach is only 'suggested by experience' this rules out the idea that by immediately perceiving a set of ideas that constitutes a *part* of the coach we perceive the coach itself. Suggestion is, of course, an instance of *mediate* perception, and this seems to cut against the suggestion that coaches and other objects are immediately perceived.[21] But I think what Philonous says is consistent with what we have said about the immediate perception of sensible objects. What happens in cases of mediate perception – inference and suggestion – is that the perceiver comes to form *judgements*, either conscious or unconscious, about what they do not immediately perceive on the basis of what they do immediately perceive. In the coach case, on this reconstruction, we immediately perceive a set of sensible qualities that constitute a part of the coach, but because of suggestion we also form a judgement *that* this is a subset of the set of qualities that constitute a coach, and mediately perceive *that* there is a coach in the street.

It is the fact that we draw inferences from what we immediately perceive that allows Berkeley to respond to another objection to his account of perception. Objects are the immediate objects of sense and we can make no mistakes about what we immediately perceive. However, we are subject to a number of perceptual illusions. But how is this possible? Hylas puts the point to Philonous with the following question: if we are to judge the reality of things by our senses, 'how can a man be mistaken in thinking the moon a plain lucid surface, about a foot in diameter; or a square tower, seen at a distance, round; or an oar, with one end in water, crooked?' (DHP3 238). How can it be that the oar looks crooked even though in reality it is not? Philonous responds by stating that the object of immediate perception *is* crooked. Where we go wrong is in the inferences we draw from what we immediately perceive. So, I see the crooked oar and I assume that this set of ideas is part of a larger set that includes its looking crooked when it is not in the water. But it is actually a

---

[21] Cf. Chapter 4, section 3, pp. 57–62.

member of a different set of ideas that constitute the oar, which includes its looking straight when it is out of the water.

Let us now turn to the issue of interpersonal perception. Can you and I perceive numerically the same object? It might be thought that Berkeley's answer to the question will decide between the IS and EP interpretation because of the following. On the IS interpretation of the mind-dependence of sensible qualities interpersonal perception seems impossible. The immediate objects of awareness are private sensations. When you and I perceive the 'same' object you are aware of your sensation and I am aware of mine. The two sets of sensations have a common cause, of course – both are caused by God. But this is akin to our both been kicked in the shin by the same person, whereby you and I undergo numerically distinct experiences that just happen to be caused by the same person. Matters look more promising on the EP interpretation. Sensible objects are essentially appearances whose existence depends on the active perception of God. Such objects are nevertheless independent of particular finite minds, and so there is no evident reason why one and the same object cannot be an appearance both for your mind and for mine. Sensible objects on this view are 'public'. So in light of this one might expect that what Berkeley says about interpersonal perception would point unequivocally in one direction or the other. Unfortunately, matters are not straightforward.

Hylas approaches the issue by asking Philonous the following:

HYLAS: Is it not your opinion that by our senses we perceive only the ideas existing in our minds?
PHILONOUS: It is.
HYLAS: But the same idea which is my mind, cannot be in yours, or in any other mind. Doth it not follow from your principles that no two can see the same thing? And is this not highly absurd?

(DHP3 247)

Philonous' reply runs as follows. He says that if we stick to the 'vulgar acceptation' of 'same', then two or more persons can be said to see the same thing. If, however:

the term *same* be used in the acceptation of the philosophers, then, according to their sundry definitions (for it is not yet agreed wherein that philosophic identity consists), it may or may not be possible for divers persons to perceive the same thing. But whether philosophers shall think fit to call a thing the *same* or no, is, I conceive, of small importance. (DHP3 247)

How does this help? One way to read it is as follows.[22] Philonous agrees with Hylas on the assumption that minds cannot share ideas. To accommodate interpersonal perception – or rather something like it – we should understand the distinction between the vulgar and philosophic sense of 'the same' as the distinction between *qualitative* and *numerical* identity. Roughly, qualitative identity is a relation between distinct things or items that nevertheless share the same properties. So, if you and I both have a copy of the 1711 edition of Berkeley's *Principles* we have each a copy of the same book. Numerical identity is not a relation between two things. In numerical identity there is just one thing. Hylas is asking whether you and I perceive numerically the same thing. Philonous, on this reading, rejects numerical identity as a mere fiction of philosophy, claiming we perceive two *qualitatively* identical things. In the book example, you and I are affected qualitatively by the same or similar sensations and so perceive qualitatively the same thing.

If this is Berkeley's response it is pretty hopeless.[23] The distinction between qualitative and numerical identity is a commonsensical one. We can easily distinguish between, say, the ten copies of Berkeley's *Principles* in the bookshop and your particular copy. Berkeley would be trying to evade the objection by making a very implausible claim about the common-sense notion of identity. However, this implausible reading is partly premised on a mistaken view about what is the source of the problem of interpersonal perception. It assumes that it must be generated by the alleged privacy of ideas (that ideas are private sensations). I cannot 'see' your ideas and you cannot 'see' mine, and so there is a problem about how we can see the same thing. But, following Richard Glauser, I think the issue that is dealt with in this exchange does not really turn on the issue of privacy.[24] We might think it does because Philonous does not contradict Hylas' claim that the 'same idea which is [in] my mind, cannot be in yours, or in any other mind'. The EP interpretation allows that sensible qualities (ideas) are 'public', so that you and I can perceive numerically the

[22] See, e.g., Fogelin, *Berkeley and the* Principles of Human Knowledge, pp. 91–2.
[23] As Fogelin points out in *Berkeley and the* Principles of Human Knowledge, pp. 91–2.
[24] Richard Glauser, 'Berkeley on the Numerical Identity of what Several Immediately Perceive (Three Dialogues between Hylas and Philonous III 247–8)', *Philosophy Compass*, 7/8 (2012), 517–30.

same sensible quality. This does not conflict with Hylas' claim that 'we perceive only our ideas' when this is properly understood. Any sensible quality is essentially an appearance. That is what constitutes its status as an idea, that is, an object before the mind. When it is an appearance for you, then it is *your* idea. It is related to your mind. But that very same appearance could be an appearance for me too. So you and I could perceive numerically the same idea. The quality of red that I now perceive is subsequently perceived by you.

Philonous does not, however, contradict Hylas on whether the same idea can be in more than one mind. The reason why he does not is because that fact is irrelevant to the real problem. For the problem concerns not whether we perceive the same idea, but whether we see the same *object*, that is, the relevant collection of sensible qualities. Why? The question of whether you and I perceive the same *object* depends upon whether the set of sensory ideas I presently enjoy is or is not a subset of the sensory qualities that compose the object that you perceive. That is going to depend on whether we are both more or less prepared to treat the same collection of sensible qualities as members of the same thing. The reason to think that this is the issue at hand is that it makes sense of what Philonous actually says in response. As we noted, Philonous replies by drawing a distinction between vulgar and abstract notions of identity, and I suggested above that he rejects an abstract notion of identity because he holds that no sense can be made of identity criteria independently of the particular kind of object we have in mind. So, in the vulgar sense of being identical we can see numerically the same thing once we agree which set of sensible qualities are constitutive of it. Thus, Philonous says we should 'suppose several men together, all endued with the same faculties, and consequently affected in like sort by their senses, and who had yet never known the use of language; they would without question agree in their perceptions'. Here we have a situation where we have the same ideas, but have yet to bundle those ideas into objects. But 'when they came to the use of speech, some regarding the uniformness of what they perceived, might call it the same *thing*; others especially regarding the diversity of persons who perceived, might choose the denomination of different things' (DHP3 247–8). The sensible qualities that I might choose to collect under a single term as a 'thing' you might treat differently, that is, as not constituting the same thing. The problem about seeing the same thing stems from the fact that our sensory experience varies greatly from person to person, and whether we see the same thing will depend on whether we agree to bundle sensible qualities similarly. Philonous presses this point by discussing the question of identity through change, using the example of the house discussed above. Whether or not it is the same house depends on whether we share the same notions.

Philonous also tells Hylas that the problem equally affects materialists. For they immediately perceive only ideas. So there is a further question about whether, given the diversity in experience, you and I can be said to perceive the same thing. The difference between Philonous and the materialist would be that whereas Philonous holds that it is us who bundle qualities into objects, the materialist holds that the bundling is determined by the substance itself. They suppose, as Hylas puts it, 'an external archetype, to which referring their several ideas'. Philonous, somewhat unenthusiastically, allows that his system could allow for such archetypes that serve 'all the ends of identity'. These are ideas in the mind of God that would unify one set of ideas as a single thing. But Berkeley himself believed no such thing, since he thought the individuation of the timeless world of sensible qualities was an altogether human affair.

7 CONCLUSION

What, then, is the real world in Berkeley's system? It is not, as the IS interpretation of mind-dependence might encourage, a theistically orchestrated sequence of subjective or private sensations occurring in the minds of finite spirits. Instead, it is constituted by a vast array of inert sensible qualities, the existence of which is determined by the active perception of God. These actualities become reality for us when God exhibits them to finite minds. The real world is independent of our particular finite minds and continues to exist independently of them as well. We can perceive numerically the same things once we agree how to divide these sensory qualities into objects, and we can perceive objects rather than just sensory qualities. The world is just how it seems to be.

One might take issue with Berkeley by saying that we do not think of objects as mere collections of qualities whose grouping owes itself merely to human interests and decisions. A stone or any other physical object is a genuine unity because it is a discrete *loci* of causal inter-action. I think in terms of stones because those qualities are united by the fact that they have various effects on the world, and not because of some arbitrary decision to name a set of qualities as 'stone'. Science gets to the bottom of things by revealing how things are causally related and what powers are distinctive of kinds of things. In the next chapter we will examine Berkeley's radical departure from this picture.

CHAPTER 7

Science and mathematics

I INTRODUCTION

In the sequence of sections §§34–84, Berkeley considers a host of objections to his system. Some of these we have already discussed while addressing other topics, such as continuity. Other objections concern the compatibility of Berkeley's system with orthodox religion. He considers, to give a couple of examples, the claim that the existence of matter is supported by the Bible (PHK §82) and whether his system allows for miracles (PHK §84). Yet another family of objections represents various attempts to rehabilitate the notion of material substance (PHK §§67–81). We shall not, however, consider these objections nor Berkeley's replies to them; instead, we shall consider objections, contained in PHK §§50–66, that concern the compatibility of immaterialism with the practice of science. Berkeley is acutely aware that the rise of modern science is a point of pride for the philosophers of the period, and that immaterialism seems to threaten its very intelligibility. His replies to these objections inform a general account of the practice of science developed later in the *Principles*, an account he views as superior to that available to materialism. He also thinks that his philosophy is advantageous to the formal science of mathematics.

The overall aim of this chapter is to sketch Berkeley's philosophy of science and mathematics as presented in the *Principles*. We will begin examining Berkeley's account of science by considering how he deals with the objection that his philosophy removes all natural causality from the world (§7.2). His response to this objection is interesting because, although he holds that all talk that attributes causal powers to objects is false, he nevertheless claims that we may continue to talk

116

that way. This view rests ultimately on the surprising thesis that natural events are not related by cause and effect, but instead stand in *semantic* relations of *sign* and *signified*. The natural world thereby constitutes the language by which God communicates with finite creatures. For example, fire does not *cause* burning, fire is a *sign* for burning, just as a red cross is a sign for medical aid. This thesis is also employed to rebut another objection to Berkeley's system: if things are just collections of ideas revealed by God, why then do many of them have highly complex inner structures? In discussing this objection to Berkeley's system, we shall also discuss the wider issue of whether Berkeley thought science was aimed at truth or merely at offering accounts that yield useful predictions. Finally, we will look briefly at the view of mathematics Berkeley advances in the *Principles*.

2 CAUSAL TALK AND THE LANGUAGE OF GOD

If things are ideas and ideas are passive, then there are no natural causes – only spirits are causes, and physical objects are all inert. But is this not absurd? We must 'no longer say upon these [that is, Berkeley's] principles that fire heats, or water cools' (PHK §51). Berkeley allows that this does seem absurd. Our language is shot through with causal terms that apply to natural objects such as 'scratch', 'burn', 'break' and so on, and, if we follow Berkeley's view, describing the world in these terms is mistaken. All statements that attribute causal efficacy to physical objects are false when taken 'in a strict and speculative sense' (PHK §51). But Berkeley does not recommend that we should give up talking in this way. We should, as Berkeley famously puts it, 'think with the learned, and speak with the vulgar' (PHK §51). We should not hold that such statements that ascribe causal properties to objects are true, but we may nevertheless continue to talk in this way.

But why? If saying that fire burns, knives cut and saws saw involves an error, then why not give up talking that way? Perhaps it is just too difficult to stop talking in these terms. However, that is not Berkeley's position. Instead, he says such phrases 'may be retained, so long as they excite in us proper sentiments, or dispositions to act in such a manner as is necessary for our well-being' (PHK §52). This should remind us of Berkeley's comments in his Introduction about the various functions of language. The ends of language include not merely the communication of ideas, but also 'the raising of some passion, the exciting to, or deterring from an action, [and] the putting the mind in some particular disposition' (PHK I §20). So the following seems to be on the cards: even though causal utterances are false, such utterances are acceptable if the primary intention in uttering them is some end other than the mere conveyance of information, such as helping the hearer to avoid something or arousing in him or her some emotion. I might say to you 'the pan will burn you', not with the primary intention of communicating to you the fact that the pan is hot, but to prevent you from touching it and hurting yourself. Again, I might say to you 'the wine will relax you', not with the primary intention of conveying that fact, but to elicit your approval of the wine. Such utterances perform a legitimate linguistic function even though they are false.

This is the core of Berkeley's defence of the vulgar use of causal talk, but what we have said thus far is too piecemeal. What gives this idea a more systematic character is Berkeley's claim about the relation between ideas, given that it is not causal. This claim is made at PHK §65, where Berkeley tells us that the relation between ideas or things – which we mistakenly take to be one of cause and effect – is actually a relation of *sign* and *signified*: 'The fire which I see is not the cause of the pain I suffer upon my approaching it, but the mark that forewarns me of it.' Fundamentally, relations among ideas are not causal but semantic, and the system of nature constitutes the language by which God communicates with finite creatures. This connects with Berkeley's claim that we can retain causal talk in the following way: causal phrases can be retained because they tend to elicit responses in subjects that are generally similar to the responses that God is trying to elicit in us by his natural utterances. If I tell you 'fire causes pain' you avoid the fire, so I elicit in you a behaviour that God is trying to elicit in you in his making fire a sign *for* pain. To explore this thought further, let us first try to understand the idea that natural events constitute a language.

A useful entry point to understanding this claim, which I borrow from Jonathan Dancy,[1] is the distinction drawn by H. P. Grice

---

[1] Jonathan Dancy, *Berkeley: An Introduction* (Oxford: Blackwell, 1987), p. 116.

between 'natural' and 'non-natural' or 'conventional' meaning.[2] Suppose, *contra* Berkeley, that there are causal relations among natural events. We can use our knowledge of causal relations to infer either the cause from the effect or predict the effect from the cause. If I see certain paw prints in the snow in my garden, I can infer from their presence that a fox has recently been there. Conversely, if I know that heating ice causes it to melt, I can predict that it will do so when I apply heat to it. Knowledge of cause and effect enables me to infer from something I presently observe to something I do not presently observe, be it effect from cause or cause to effect. We often use the expression 'means' in connection with such inferences. I know that there was a fox in the garden because those paw prints *mean* that there has been one there. I know the ice will melt because the temperature in the room *means* that it will melt. This is the sense in which meaning can be 'natural'. *Non-natural* meaning is where there is a relation between a symbol and a thing that is constituted by an arbitrary but stable convention instituted by the intentions of speakers. So, in the English language, the word 'cat', in either its spoken or written forms, is used to refer to cats, but there is nothing in nature that dictates that this word rather than any other should be used as a sign for cats. It is, rather, that the noise or written token is fixed by convention as meaning (referring to) cats. When we know what the sign or symbol means we understand to what it refers.

Evidently a language constituted by conventional meanings is an immensely complicated structure, but what is important for our concerns is that Berkeley takes the relations between ideas that we mistakenly take to be *causal* to be relations of conventional meaning. Just as a road sign can forewarn one of a dangerous turn, the visual idea of the fire forewarns one of pain. And, just as I come to understand what the road sign means by knowing of what it warns me, I come to understand what the visual ideas of fire mean by understanding that they warn me of fire. When God speaks the language of nature to us his intention is more than the mere conveyance of information. The particular visual experience of fire that is constitutive of the pain 'utterance' need not simply tell us of the potential pain, but encourage us to avoid it. It is an instance of using language for exciting or deterring

---

[2] H. P. Grice, 'Meaning', *Philosophical Review* 66 (1957), 377–88.

action. Since God is trying to instil in us the appropriate dispositions through the system of signs and signified that constitute nature, then it is not surprising that causal phrases may be retained if they too elicit the right dispositions. For although when I say 'fire causes pain' I say something false 'in a strict and speculative sense' if I nevertheless deter you from putting your hand in the fire, you are put in a state that is equivalent to understanding what God is trying to convey by making fire a sign for pain.

Berkeley does not work any of this out in detail in the *Principles*. However, his view on the status of causal talk anticipates what contemporary philosophers call 'fictionalism'.[3] Fictionalism concerns how we should understand thought and talk in areas that philosophers have found traditionally problematic. Roughly put, it is the claim that areas of discourse, though false, can nevertheless be retained because the aim in using it is something other than uttering the truth. Consider, for example, our talk about numbers. On the face of it sentences like '2 + 2 = 4' refer to abstract objects that exist in a platonic realm. Since there *are* no abstract objects, then it seems that mathematical statements are all false, since they presuppose a subject matter that does not exist. Does this mean that we should stop doing mathematics or stop talking about numbers? According to fictionalism, the answer to this question is 'no'. Instead, we should just not take such talk literally. We can continue to talk 'as if' there are numbers because doing so is a useful fiction. One version of fictionalism holds that our typical use of such sentences is non-literal and that we use such sentences to perform other functions. This is called 'hermeneutic fictionalism'.[4] *Revolutionary* fictionalism suggests that we *ought* to treat such sentences non-literally and think of them as having a function other that stating facts about causal relations. Thus, we '*ought* to think with the learned, and speak with the vulgar' (PHK §51, added emphasis). If this is to work then, quite apart from

[3] On fictionalism in general, see the papers in Mark Kalderon (ed.), *Fictionalism in Metaphysics* (Oxford: Clarendon Press, 2005), and in connection with Berkeley, see P. J. E. Kail, 'Causation, Fictionalism and Non-Cognitivism', in S. Parigi (ed.), *George Berkeley: Religion and Science in the Age of Enlightenment* (Dordrecht: Springer, 2010), pp. 31–40.

[4] On hermeneutic and revolutionary fictionalisms, see Jason Stanley, 'Hermeneutic Fictionalism', in P. French and H. Wettstein (eds.), *Midwest Studies in Philosophy* xxv: *Figurative Language* (Oxford: Blackwell, 2001), pp. 36–71. Stanley finds hermeneutic fictionalism implausible.

Berkeley's general position on the language of God, we need to be confident that a significant number of our everyday uses of causal phrases are such as to direct action or elicit other responses in the listener, albeit in complicated ways. It is clear that sometimes we do use causal phrases in this way; for example, if I tell you that my two-year-old son is a biter, I can be telling you this to be on your guard when you give him a cuddle. Whether, however, this generalises to all or most of our causal phrases is quite another matter, and one which I shall leave the reader to consider.

3 SCIENCE, COMPLEXITY AND UNDERSTANDING

Berkeley is acutely aware that by dispensing with natural causality he is leaving himself open to the charge of denying that there is any room for scientific explanation (PHK §50). Mechanical science promised a way of explaining the behaviour of the physical world in terms of matter in motion. Questions of the form 'why did *x* occur?' could be answered in terms of citing the *efficient* cause of the event *x*, the cause, that is, that brings *x* about. How that event is brought about – the nature of the efficient cause – is to be understood in terms of the impact of one body upon another and the transfer of motion from the one to the other. Such particular transactions could be subsumed under general and relatively simple laws of motion. But the initial optimism of this picture was quickly lost for a whole host of reasons, one of which was trying to make sense of the active powers of material objects.[5] Malebranche's response to this problem was occasionalism. Material objects have no active powers and all genuine efficacy resides in God. Berkeley responds to this idea by stating that this would mean that God must therefore create matter for 'no manner of purpose', which is an 'unaccountable and extravagant supposition' (PHK §53). Locke, on the other hand, took refuge in metaphysical modesty. We do not understand *how* bodies causally affect one another, he said, but nevertheless we can generalise from experience and observation, and in turn explain and predict other events in light of these generalisations. Locke's account still explains events causally, even if the nature of causation is hidden to us. This mixture of modesty and

---

[5] Cf. Chapter 2, section 6, pp. 29–31.

mechanics was crowned by Sir Isaac Newton's *Principia Mathematica* (first published in 1687). It is difficult to overestimate the significance of Newton's achievement, and Berkeley does not deny it, writing at PHK §110 that the 'best key for ... natural science, will be easily acknowledged to be a certain celebrated treatise of *mechanics*'. Towards the end of this section we will discuss Berkeley's attitude to some of the particular features of Newton's natural philosophy. First, however, let us make some general remarks about Berkeley's philosophy of science.

Berkeley agrees that science is in the business of deriving generalisations from observation. However, this scientific approach does not yield 'knowledge of the efficient cause that produces' effects, but instead yields 'greater largeness of comprehension, whereby analogies, harmonies, and agreements are discovered in the works of Nature, and the particular effects are explained, that is, reduced to, general rules' (PHK §105). This last part of Berkeley's statement suggests that he does not really hold that science *explains* natural events, because science really *reduces* particular effects to rules. On the Lockean model, science explains because it informs us of the causes that are operative in particular kinds of events, and so when we consider some particular event we can explain why it happened by saying that it has such and such a cause. But by 'reducing' particular events to such and such a regularity, Berkeley's scientist seems to be merely recording that things of one kind are *followed* by things of another kind, yet the scientist cannot say *why* this is so. Nevertheless, such regularities ground predictions; they 'extend our prospect beyond what is present, and near to us, and enable us to make very probable conjectures, touching things that may have happened at very great distances of time and place, as well as to predict things to come' (PHK §105).

This emphasis on prediction, and the absence of causal explanation in Berkeley's text, might suggest that his philosophy of science is a form of *instrumentalism*. Instrumentalism is a creature of the late nineteenth and twentieth centuries, and admits of many and subtle variations, but, at a first approximation, according to instrumentalism, as W. H. Newton-Smith puts it:

the aim of the scientific enterprise is merely the production of theories that are empirically adequate in the sense that they give successful observational predications. The question of the truth of the theoretical postulates of science simply does not arise. The only proper concern of the scientist is that those postulates give rise to correct predications.[6]

There is something right as well as something wrong in this view of Berkeley. What is right concerns the 'theoretical postulates' of science, and we shall discuss what this means presently. But if it is thought that the only proper concern of science is mere predication, rather than attempting to *understand* the natural world, then it is at least as misleading as a characterisation of Berkeley. Why? Much earlier in the *Principles* Berkeley responds to the accusation that his system leaves no room for explanation by saying that to explain any phenomenon is 'to show why upon such and such occasions we are affected with such and such ideas' (PHK §50). Locke had attempted to answer such 'why' questions by citing efficient causes. But one might answer why questions by instead appealing to *final* causes. A final cause is, roughly, the goal or end of some happening. So when asked why I am going for a walk, I reply that I am doing so for the sake of my health. The final cause of my walking is therefore health. In PHK §108, Berkeley tells us that we can answer questions of the kind 'why did such and such happen?' by pointing out 'the various ends, to which natural things are adapted, and for which they were originally with unspeakable wisdom contrived'. Laws are 'not the result of any immutable habitudes, or relations betweens things themselves, but only of God's goodness and kindness to men in the administration of the world'. Since natural events are the direct result of God's will, and not the effects of a blind mechanism, we are secure in the assumption that events occur with some aim in view. So, at least in principle, science can aspire to explanations of natural events that advert to what God is aiming at in establishing such and such laws.

Nevertheless, the postulation of final causes is not central to Berkeley's account. God's aims are general ones, like the promotion of the wellbeing of humanity, and cannot really help in connection with the specific regularities that constitute the laws of nature. These regularities are not simply brute, but are the rules that both constitute

---

[6] William H. Newton-Smith, 'Berkeley's Philosophy of Science', in J. Foster and H. Robinson (eds.), *Essays on Berkeley: A Tercentennial Celebration* (Oxford: Clarendon Press, 1985), p. 149.

and govern the language of God that, in turn, constitutes the natural world. This allows science to aspire to more than mere prediction; science can aspire to *interpretation*. In the 1710 edition of the *Principles*, Berkeley writes that there are 'two ways of learning a language, either by rule or by practice: a man may be well read in the language of Nature, without understanding the grammar of it, or being able to say by what rule a thing is so or so' (PHK §108). The first part of this claim picks up on the ordinary person's relation to the natural world. In one sense ordinary people do understand the world in the sense that when they make predictions and act appropriately they are acting just as if they understand that God is communicating to them. A metaphysician like Berkeley, however, knows that the relations we deem causal are really semantic ones. The scientist can know this too and his understanding is of the second kind – he transforms the pre-theoretical understanding of the world into an understanding of the rules by which God's language is governed, and comes to know the meaning of the God's utterances.

This view of the aims of science and the rule-governed nature of God's language come together in Berkeley's answer to another objection voiced at PHK §60. We know that there is a great deal of complexity in the natural world. Plants and animals, for example, have immensely complex internal structures – yet a good deal of this structure and complexity is typically something we do not perceive. Why this hidden complexity? If the world is a sequence of ideas caused by God, is there any need for plants and animals and the rest of creation to have inner workings, especially since such unobserved workings are causally impotent? This objection relates to the practice of science, since science investigates the internal structures of things, and this is particularly worrisome for Berkeley as the range of observable phenomena widened in the early modern period with the invention of the microscope and the telescope. Both instruments revealed to human beings a realm of things that were previously unperceived. Telescopes revealed the rings of Saturn and the imperfections on the moon, a body previously thought to be a perfect sphere; while microscopes revealed tiny organisms living in water and the fine structure of leaves.

Berkeley's response has the following shape: any language with which we are familiar comprises a finite vocabulary, and a finite set of rules governing its usage. The rules determine how the vocabulary can be combined to form meaningful sentences. What a sentence means is partly a function of the words it contains and partly a function of its structure, a structure that expresses the rules of composition. The sentence 'the man bites the dog' is a different sentence from 'the dog bites the man' even though both sentences contain the same words. Now languages can have a great deal of expressive power in that a finite set of rules and a finite vocabulary can equip one to express a vast variety of different thoughts. This is because the meanings of sentences depend systematically on both rules and vocabulary, and these are vital for our capacity to generate and understand new sentences. Without this feature, our capacity to compose new sentences and to understand them becomes inexplicable. At the same time, in order to express any complex thought in that language I must be constrained by rules that govern the composition of sentences. So, in order to express the thought 'the black cat sat cleaning his paws on the mat after eating some fish', I need to respect the rules that determine the composition of its elements. Thus, I use the words 'black' and 'cat' to express 'black cat' and place that expression in a certain position to determine that it is the subject of the sentence. Now, in the language of God there is a large but presumably finite stock of idea-types. These can be combined to make more complex signs, analogous to English sentences built up from the finite stock of English words, according to the rules that govern correct composition. Given that nature constitutes a language, the complex signs we perceive on a day-to-day basis (the tree outside my front door, for example) must be the product of a finite vocabulary and the rules governing it. It is this that explains why there are inner structures that are contingently unobserved. The

reason why ideas are formed into machines, that is, artificial and regular combinations, is the same with that for combining letters into words. That a few original ideas may be made to signify a great number of effects and actions, it is necessary that they be variously combined together: and to the end their use by permanent and universal, these combinations must be made by *rule*, and with *wise contrivance*. (PHK §65)

Berkeley's talk about the combining of letters into words is unfortunate. The ways in which letters combine to make words is entirely different from the way in which words combine to form new sentences. However, we should let that pass, since Berkeley can still make his point in the same way that we are making it. In investigating the complexity of the world, especially and including the inner structure of natural objects, we are coming to understand the general rules by which the language of God is governed, which in turn helps us to interpret the meaning of particular events.

It must be admitted, however, that Berkeley's programme for science in the *Principles* is exceedingly programmatic. It is relatively easy to understand the position in the abstract and the general way it deals with the objection from complexity just considered, but difficult to know how it works in detail. One thing animating Berkeley's thinking is his ambivalent attitude to the success of modern science and, as I mentioned, in particular Newtonian mechanics. Berkeley thought that Newton's science, and Locke's underwriting of that science, brought in metaphysical and epistemological assumptions that stand in the way of the proper execution of science. Remember that one of Berkeley's aims, mentioned in the subtitle of the *Principles*, is to enquire into the 'Chief Causes of Error and Difficulty in the *Sciences*'. An obvious obstacle is one we have mentioned in a number of places, namely, the view that material substances have powers and internal structures hidden from us (PHK §101). This is the Lockean position, and it is the source of scepticism Berkeley mentions early on in his Introduction, namely, the 'the obscurity of things, or the natural weakness and imperfections of our understandings' (PHK I §2).

Berkeley also objects to Newton's claim that bodies occupy places in *absolute* space and moments in *absolute* time. Time, in Newton's view, exists independently of our perception or measurement of it, and is a 'substance' in which events occur. If things did not change, there would still exist a measure of duration of those unchanging things. Much earlier in the *Principles* (PHK §§97–8), Berkeley signals his allegiance to the claim that time is just a relation between different events, which for him are just sequences of ideas. Similarly, absolute space is conceived in the Newtonian world as a 'container' which bodies occupy. Berkeley mounts an interesting attack on absolute space at PHK §§112–17, but rather than discuss this we shall instead focus on what seems to be an oddity in his discussion, which sheds light on his philosophy of science. Since for Berkeley space is not a 'container' in which things are placed, but consists in the relations in which objects stand, the motion of an object from one place to another is relative to some other object, and not relative to absolute space. But Berkeley also distinguishes between the apparent and real motion of an object. If I stand by the road the cars pass me by, and really are in motion. However, as I sit on a moving bus, the houses appear to be moving relative to me, but they are in fact stationary. The motion of the houses is merely apparent. Berkeley is, we noted, aware of the difference between real and apparent motion, and thinks he can account for it in his system. At PHK §115 he says that for a body really to be moved requires that 'some force or action' be applied to it. So the car is really moving because of a force impressed upon it, whereas the motion of the house is only apparent. In the 1710 edition of the PHK the same section refers to an 'impressed force' and a 'power productive of change of place'. But this appears very puzzling: how can Berkeley avail himself of 'powers' or 'forces' given all that he has said about the inertness of ideas?

The answer is that Berkeley is treating terms like 'force' not as referring to genuine powers, but instead as useful fictions in science. It is in the sense that he is an instrumentalist in the philosophy of science. The use of terms like 'force' in the *Principles* looks forward to a developed theory of the use of such terms in science he offers in *De Motu* (DM) (*On Motion*) published in 1721. There he writes:

Force, gravity, attraction, and terms of this sort are useful for reasonings and computations about motion and bodies in motion, but not for understanding the simple nature of motion itself or for indicating so many distinct qualities. As for attraction, it was certainly introduced by Newton, not as a true, physical quality, but only as a mathematical hypothesis. (DM §17)

Science makes use of theoretical entities to explain observable phenomena, where, very roughly, a theoretical entity is theoretical in virtue of not being observable. One can take one of two broad attitudes to the status of such theoretical entities. One is a *realist* attitude that holds that such terms refer to genuine features of the world and so, for example, we must hold that there are forces since they explain the relevant phenomena. Instrumentalism denies that the use of such terms commits us, or is intended to commit us, to the existence of theoretical entities like forces. Instead, terms like 'force' are simply a 'way of speaking' (DM §28) that help in prediction. They are 'of first utility for theories and formulations, as also for computations about motion, even if in the truth of things, and in bodies actually existing, they would be looked for in vain, like the geometers fictions made by mathematical abstraction' (DM §39).[7] What is important in Newton's account of the world (for Berkeley) is not its apparent metaphysical commitments, but how it provides a mathematical framework for prediction. Terms like 'force' are perfectly acceptable when they are not taken as literal descriptions of reality.[8]

4 MATHEMATICS

Berkeley had a lifelong interest in mathematics, beginning with *Arithmetica et Miscellanea Mathematica*, written in support of his application for a fellowship at Trinity College. His most famous contribution is his critique of calculus presented in *The Analyst* (1734). The *Philosophical Commentaries* contain some quite radical views on arithmetic and geometry, but by the time the *Principles* was published these views had softened somewhat, though they remained radical enough.[9] Here we shall confine ourselves to a description of Berkeley's main claims.

The *Principles* considers both arithmetic (PHK §§119–22) and geometry (PHK §§123–33). The discussion of these two branches of mathematics reflects Berkeley's scepticism about abstract ideas, and the metaphysics of immaterialism greatly informs his discussion of geometry. The dominant view of mathematics in Berkeley's day

---

[7] Berkeley presents his account of the meanings of terms like 'force' in the *De Motu* as quite independent of immaterialism, and indeed it is. A materialist could consistently be an instrumentalist about forces.

[8] For an excellent discussion of Berkeley's general philosophy of science, see Lisa Downing, 'Berkeley's Natural Philosophy and Philosophy of Science', in K. Winkler (ed.), *The Cambridge Companion to Berkeley* (Cambridge University Press, 2005), pp. 230–65. Berkeley's views on science developed quite considerably throughout his lifetime, and Downing's article gives a sense of this development.

[9] The standard and extremely useful work on Berkeley's mathematics is Jesseph, *Berkeley's Philosophy of Mathematics*. A shorter presentation of its main themes is to be found in Douglas Jesseph, 'Berkeley's Philosophy of Mathematics', in K. Winkler (ed.), *The Cambridge Companion to Berkeley* (Cambridge University Press, 2005), pp. 266–310. The present section is indebted to Jesseph's work.

derived from Aristotle's abstractionist account.[10] On this view mathematical objects, like numbers and shapes, are not independent abstract objects or platonic forms, but are constructed by forming representations that abstract away from the particularities of concrete objects. Berkeley alludes to this position at PHK §119 when he introduces the topic of arithmetic. Much earlier in the *Principles* Berkeley claims that number 'is a creature of the mind' (PHK §12), and that we have no abstract idea of unity (PHK §13). The general thought here is that there is no answer to the question 'how many *x*s are there?' independent of our counting conventions. The question 'How many objects are there in the room?' depends on what we are prepared to count as an object. Given that number is relative, then there can be no abstract idea of unity in itself.

Berkeley also holds that arithmetic is incorrectly understood as a purely speculative body of knowledge. Instead, claims Berkeley, arithmetic is nothing but an empty formal practice or manipulation of signs when considered independently of its practical use. In indirect support of this Berkeley offers a speculative genealogy of the emergence of arithmetic. For ease of memory and calculation, humans employ marks like strokes in recording units. These strokes then fall under other marks (for example, five strokes are represented by a cross). From such practices emerge notation systems like Arabic, which contain signs and rules for their manipulation that are so disciplined that they can greatly outrun the earlier primitive notation. This conjecture of how the practice of arithmetic emerges indirectly supports Berkeley inasmuch as it shows, if successful, how it is possible that we can begin talking about numbers and performing computations without the need for abstract ideas. Abstract ideas are not, therefore, needed to account for arithmetic. Independent of the particular concrete things that the signs can be used to name, arithmetic is concerned only with the signs and the rules governing their manipulation, and in this Berkeley is a forerunner of what is called 'formalism' in the philosophy of mathematics.[11] Arithmetic *per se* is

---

[10] On this background, see Jesseph, *Berkeley's Philosophy of Mathematics*, ch. 1.

[11] For critical discussion of Berkeley as a formalist, see Claire Schwartz, 'Berkeley and his Contemporaries: The Question of Mathematical Formalism', in S. Parigi (ed.), *George Berkeley: Religion and Science in the Age of Enlightenment* (Dordrecht: Springer, 2010), pp. 43–56.

simply the manipulation of signs according to rules, and those signs are not intrinsically about anything. Nevertheless, the signs and their relations can be applied to the world and used to order and guide our practice: 'In *arithmetic* therefore we regard not the *things* but the *signs*, which nevertheless are not regarded for their own sake, but because they direct us how to act with relation to things and dispose rightly of them' (PHK §122).

Geometry differs from arithmetic inasmuch as, although geometrical terms are again *signs*, we nevertheless have particular ideas that represent by resemblance properties of a particular extension or a particular triangle. We can also think about geometrical properties in general by making a particular idea stand for all ideas of the same sort (PHK I §12). The sense in which geometry is about any thing is that it is about appearances to the senses, rather than abstract geometrical entries such as triangularity *per se*. This, Berkeley thinks, helps us to avoid a notorious paradox: the paradox of infinite divisibility. For any geometric magnitude it seems possible to divide it into two equal magnitudes. One version of the paradox is then that any finite magnitude can be continuously divided so that it must be composed of an infinite number of magnitudes. But seemingly no finite thing can be composed of an infinite number of things (PHK §128). The relevance of immaterialism to this version of the paradox is as follows: extended things are ideas and, Berkeley claims, the transparent character of ideas reveals that they cannot contain innumerable parts (PHK §123). Any attempt to divide extension terminates in *minima sensibilia*, which are the smallest perceptible points. These cannot be further divided, since were they to become smaller they would cease to be perceived and so cease to exist (PHK §132).[12] The diagnosis of our propensity to be perplexed by the paradox is the misuse of a sign employed in geometrical reasoning. When reasoning about geometry we do not employ abstract ideas of the kind rejected in the Introduction, but we use a particular idea to stand for similar things. So, for example, a particular inch length can be used to stand for all length. However, when we use this line as a sign for length in general

---

[12] For some useful discussion of *minima sensibilia* in Berkeley's philosophy, see Margaret Atherton, *Berkeley's Revolution in Vision* (Ithaca, NY: Cornell University Press, 1990), pp. 115–17, 133–5.

we can talk about it as length containing say, 10,000 parts, even though it does not, because our use of it is indifferent to its particular length. Unfortunately, we mistakenly transfer features of the thing represented – a length of 10,000 parts – onto the signifier (the particular idea) as if *it* had 10,000 parts (PHK §126). This, in turn, fools us into thinking the inch length that is used as a sign for length in general can have an innumerable number of parts (PHK §127).

CHAPTER 8

Spirits

I INTRODUCTION

After discussing science and mathematics, Berkeley devotes the remaining sections of the *Principles* to topics relating mostly to spirit. PHK §§135–44 considers how we know our own spirits or selves, and §§144–9 focus on our knowledge of other spirits. In discussing this second topic, Berkeley argues that we are surer of the existence of God than we are of other finite spirits. After reconciling the existence of evil in the world with the existence of God, the final sections of the *Principles* exhort the reader to appreciate the manifest presence of God in the world. The *Principles* would be 'ineffectual', Berkeley writes, 'if by what I have said I cannot inspire my readers with a pious sense of the presence of God' (PHK §156).

I will let the reader judge whether the work is 'ineffectual' in this regard. In this chapter we shall concern ourselves with Berkeley's account of spirit or self. The brief discussion in the *Principles* of the knowledge we have of ourselves invites further questions that Berkeley does not address within the pages of that work. Or, to put it more dramatically, his brief remarks touch only upon the tip of a large and treacherous iceberg. Spirit is absolutely vital to his system and so we need an account of it – and also how we know it – if we are to be persuaded by Berkeley's philosophy. But he offers no systemic account of spirit, and we have to piece together what we can about spirits from both his notebooks and the brief discussions in his published work.

There are three key issues to consider. The first is epistemological, one of how we have knowledge of spirits, both in one's own case and in the case of other spirits. The *Principles'* treatment of self-knowledge (that is, knowledge of one's own self) is both brief and problematic. Berkeley denies that we can have an *idea* of the self, but this leaves us wondering quite how we have self-knowledge, or can conceive what a self is. For how can you think of something of which you have no idea? This problem spills over into our knowledge of other spirits. If I cannot conceive of what a self is in my own case, how can I even begin to understand, let alone know, that there are other selves? The second issue to consider is ontological. What exactly *are* 'spirits'? Berkeley tells us that a spirit is 'one simple, undivided, active being' (PHK §26), 'whose existence consists . . . in perceiving ideas and thinking' (PHK §139). He also calls spirits 'substances'. But many problems lurk behind this deceptively simple surface, and, as we shall see, some claim that Berkeley departs radically from traditional notions of minds as substances. The third issue concerns human action. Ideas caused by me are ideas of the imagination, while ideas or sensible qualities caused by God are real things. But do we not also affect the real world by our own action? How is this possible if reality is constituted by the causal efficacy of God?

We will begin by discussing the second of the three issues, namely, the ontological issue of the nature of spirit. The aim of this section is to give a flavour of the problems of trying to understand selves as substances. The next section considers the problem of self-knowledge. Berkeley, as we noted, claims that we do not have an idea of self, which in turn raises the question of how we can think about selves. As I said, the answer he gives in the *Principles* to this question is rather brief and unsatisfactory, so we shall turn to the *Dialogues*, where a slightly fuller answer is given. We will also touch briefly on some problems in connection with Berkeley's account of how we know other spirits. Finally, we shall turn to how Berkeley might accommodate human action. As we shall see, Berkeley's views on spirit seem problematic. So problematic, in fact, that one wishes the 'lost' Part II of the *Principles* had never been lost – if it was ever written at all.

2 SPIRITS AND SUBSTANCES

Berkeley quite frequently refers to spirits as 'substances' (for example, PHK §§7, 135, 139). As we noted in Chapter 2, section 2, 'substance' is associated with a number of traditional claims. First, substances are independent beings or 'that which may itself be itself'.[1] All other beings – modes or attributes – depend in some way upon substances. Substances are individuated into *kinds* in virtue of their essences or, as Descartes sometimes calls them, their principal attributes. The essence of mind is thought, the essence of material substance is extension. Neither kind of thing can exist when it lacks those properties, since it is the properties themselves that constitute what kinds of substance those substances are. Different qualities present in one object can exist in concert in virtue of being qualities of one substance, and the identity of an object is maintained through change of qualities by the persistence of that substance.

If we suppose that spirits are substances – independent beings – then the obvious candidates for the class of dependent beings are ideas. So we can start to approach the question of what a spirit is by trying to understand the relationship between minds and ideas. Are ideas modes of spiritual substance? Berkeley had criticised Locke for not being able to attach any sense to the crucial notion of 'support' in claiming that material substance supports modes or accidents (PHK §16), so Berkeley must be able to articulate the sense in which spirits 'support' ideas if he is not to fall foul of his own criticisms. The Cartesian way of spelling out dependency in terms of mode and attribute has the virtue of being more readily intelligible than Locke's gestures at 'support' and 'upholding'. An extended substance's principal attribute is extension, but that extension can be modified in a number of different ways. Being a triangle is one way in which something extended can be modified. Being triangular is not something that can exist independently of extension, though there can be extended things that lack this modification (square things, for example). So perhaps, if spirits are substances, Berkeley is thinking of the dependency of ideas in this way.

Berkeley, however, unequivocally rejects this framework. In PHK §49, he considers the objection that 'if extension and figure exist only in the mind, it follows that the mind is extended and figured; since extension is a mode or attribute, which (to speak with the Schools) is predicated of the subject in which it exists'. Being triangular is a mode

---

[1] Created substances are ultimately dependent on God since he creates them, but after he creates them they exist in their own right.

of extension and so the extension is literally triangular. So, it seems, if the idea of extension is a mode of spirit, spirit must, absurdly, be literally extended. But, Berkeley tells us:

qualities are in the mind only as they are perceived by it, that is, not by way of *mode* or *attribute*, but only by way of *idea*; and it no more follows that the soul or mind is extended because extension exists in it alone, than it does that it is red or blue, because those colours are on all hands acknowledged to exist in it, and nowhere else.[2]

Berkeley's rejection of the claim that the dependency of ideas on minds is that of mode and attribute is not surprising if the relevant sense of mind-dependency is as the EP interpretation has it. There is 'no substratum of . . . qualities but spirit, in which they exist, *not by way of mode or property* but as a thing perceived in that which perceives it' (DHP3 237, added emphasis).[3] Sensible objects are mind-dependent in the sense that the qualities that compose them are essentially and exhaustively appearances, and so cannot be understood independently of their appearing to minds. But they are *distinct from* or *independent of* the particular minds that perceive them; that is, ideas do not exist 'in the mind' in the sense in which they are modes of that mind. If this were true they could not be distinct from particular minds.

The claim that ideas are distinct from minds is called by Colin Turbayne the 'Distinction Principle'.[4] The Distinction Principle, however, conflicts with another thing Berkeley seems to say about the relation of ideas to minds, something that appears to point to the conclusion that Berkeley must really accept, contrary to his explicit statements otherwise: that ideas *are* modes of spiritual substance. Recall that at PHK §5 Berkeley states that we cannot abstract the existence of a sensible object – a collection of ideas – from perception.

---

[2] This last statement is an allusion to Nicolas Malebranche, who held that because colours are not qualities of physical objects, the distinctive reds and blues we experience must be modifications of something else, namely, the soul.

[3] The ideas of the imagination are also causally dependent on finite minds, in that they can be created by acts of will.

[4] Colin Turbayne (ed.), 'Lending a Hand to Philonous: The Berkeley, Plato, Aristotle Connection', in *Berkeley: Critical and Interpretative Essays* (Manchester University Press, 1982), pp. 295–310. For a good critical discussion, see A. C. Grayling, *Berkeley: The Central Arguments* (La Salle, IL: Open Court, 1986), pp. 168–74.

We cannot 'distinguish the existence of sensible objects from their being perceived', and, Berkeley adds, one 'might as easily divide a thing from itself'. Turbayne interprets this as meaning that the 'perceiving of an idea is *not distinct from the idea* perceived'. He christens this Berkeley's 'Identity Principle'.[5] The Identity Principle can be used to mount an argument that ideas must be modes of substances. The first move in this argument is the (relatively) unproblematic claim that *events* of *perceiving* are things that are not independent of particular minds. You and I can see the same object, but your perceiving the object is an event in you and my perceiving of the same object is an event in me, even though the object itself is distinct from these events of perceiving. But if the Identity Principle is correct, ideas are *not* distinct from particular events of perceiving. Ideas are identical to particular events of perceiving in particular minds, and so the best way to think of ideas is that they are modes of spirits. Ideas therefore 'exist in minds' in the sense that they inhere in minds as modes and attributes supposedly inhere in substances.[6] This view also dovetails well with the IS interpretation of mind-dependence. If ideas are merely sensations, then it seems plausible to think of ideas as dependent in the sense of being modes of spiritual substance.

We have rejected the IS interpretation of mind-dependence, and I think we should also reject the so-called Identity Principle, since the text we mentioned just now does not really support it at all. When Berkeley claims that we cannot distinguish the existence of sensible objects from their being perceived, he is not claiming that ideas are *identical* with events of perception. It is rather that there is a necessary connection between perception and ideas, so that perception cannot exist without ideas and ideas cannot exist without perception. Any *act* of perception necessarily requires an *object* towards which it is directed. Perceiving is thus, essentially, a relation *to* something and there is no perception if there is no object to perceive. Conversely, since ideas are essentially appearances they exist only when they appear *to* a perceiver.

---

[5] Turbayne, 'Lending a Hand to Philonous', p. 296.

[6] Turbayne in fact claims to identify a third principle, namely, the 'Inherence Principle', which is based on Berkeley's frequent claim that ideas 'exist only in the mind'. However, interpreting 'existing in the mind' as *inherence* is tendentious, given the EP interpretation of mind-dependence. 'Inherence' suggests an interpretation of dependency as that of mode of substance, which is unwarranted on the EP interpretation.

But this perceiver-dependence does not imply that particular acts of perception are identical with ideas, or that ideas are identical with particular acts of perception. So ideas are dependent on spirits, but not in the sense that they are modes of substances.

Does that therefore mean that spirits are not substances? Well, the discussion has introduced another candidate for modes, namely, events or acts of *perceiving*. Spirits could still be substances, the essence of which is to perceive, and whose particular modes are perceptions. This is consonant with Berkeley's statement that a spirit 'is an active being, whose existence . . . [consists] in perceiving ideas and thinking' (PHK §139). This statement also brings us to something central to Berkeley's account of spirit. Spirit is essentially *active*. This causes problems for the way we can represent spirits to ourselves that we shall take up in the next section, but it presents two other, more immediate, problems. The first is that spirits are surely active in a sense wider than simply perceiving. For example, do we not also will things and act in the world? The existence of the mind cannot simply consist in perceiving ideas and thinking. Secondly, how can perception be a form of activity, given that one key thing that is emphasised in immediate perception is that we are *passive*?

Let us begin with the second of the objections. I think the best way to think about the passivity involved in immediate perception is that we do not *create* or *bring into existence* the object perceived, and thus we are passive because the objects perceived are causally independent of us. Yet this is not in conflict with perception being *active* in that our conscious awareness of an object necessarily involves *understanding*: 'A spirit is one simple, undivided, active being: as it perceives ideas, it is called the *understanding*' (PHK §27). If we take understanding to be something that someone *does* rather than something that simply happens to her or him, then perception is active.[7] One might also think in terms of the power of discriminating or judging objects and qualities, a power present in particular acts of perception. Thus, in the notebooks Berkeley writes that in perception we 'must not altogether be Passive, there must be a disposition to act, there must be assent, w^ch

[7] See Phillip D. Cummins, 'Perceiving and Berkeley's Theory of Substance', in S. Daniel (ed.), *Reexamining Berkeley's Philosophy* (University of Toronto Press, 2007), p. 141.

is active, nay w^t do I talk There must be Actual Volition' (PC 777).[8]
So, the activity in immediate perception is the understanding or
cognition of objects that are not our own creations.

This suggestion might help us to evade an objection that stems
from an exchange in the *Dialogues*, where Philonous appears to reject
any distinction between the mental act of perception and the object of
any such act. Hylas distinguishes between a mental act and a sensation
in an attempt to secure the mind-independence of sensible objects
(DHP1 195–7). Acts, both he and Philonous agree, are mental – but
objects need not be. So with this in mind we can conceive of act
without object. Philonous asks Hylas what activity is, and Hylas
responds that the mind is active only in the exercise of the will.
Examples of actions of will include things like picking a flower and
inhaling its scent. But, says Philonous, when we perceive there is
ultimately nothing for the will to do, we are 'in the very perception . . .
altogether passive' (DHP1 197). Does this not mean that Philonous
rejects the claim that perception is a mental act? Though things are far
from unequivocal, the text does not in fact imply such a rejection. It is
not Philonous but Hylas who claims that all activity is willing, so one
might follow Phillip Cummins, who suggests that Philonous silently
holds that there is a distinct activity of perceiving, but exploits Hylas'
instance that all activity is volition for the purposes of argument.[9]

The second objection to viewing spirits as substances whose essence
is the activity of perceiving is that there is more to the mind than
perceiving. A spirit does not just perceive, it also wills. A mind is
active, says Hylas, when it 'produces, puts an end to, or changes
anything' (DHP1 196). We can treat one form of willing – namely,
the production of ideas – as an active form of *perception*. When I
imagine I am enjoying ideas, in that sense I am actively participating
in the creation of ideas. This is also the sense in which God perceives
sensible objects, as Berkeley states, 'This making . . . of ideas doth very
properly denominate the mind active' (PHK 28). But the will is wider
in scope than the creation of ideas. It can also change and destroy

---

[8] See also Stephen H. Daniel (ed.), 'Berkeley's Stoic Notion of Spiritual Substance', in *New
Interpretations of Berkeley's Thought* (Amherst, NY: Humanity Books, 2008), p. 213, who
understands activity in terms of the mind's 'differentiation' of presented ideas.

[9] See Cummins, 'Perceiving and Berkeley's Theory of Substance', pp. 141–6.

ideas, and here the notion of willing as a form of active perception seems to be overstretched. If spirit is a substance, then its essence must be activity *per se*, rather than the activity of perceiving.

We are examining the question of whether it is right to think of spirits as substances. Is it right to think of acts as modes of substance? We said that Berkeley rejects the claim that *ideas* are modes of substance, but we left open the possibility that acts are modes. However, at PHK §49, Berkeley seems to reject the whole framework of modes and substances. What philosophers say of 'subject and mode' is 'very groundless and unintelligible', a claim that seems to apply not merely to material substance but of the very notion of substance in general. One might now wonder whether there is any genuine sense of substance left in Berkeley's work. Spirits might be active, and actions include both volitions and perceptions, but what is the relation between these acts and the 'thing' or substance of which they are acts when the traditional notion of mode and subject is 'unintelligible'?

According to some commentators, Berkeley in fact quietly rejects the notion of the self as substance.[10] The self, according to one version of this view, is a system of activities all related to the ideas that are the objects of those activities. There is no thing distinct from these activities that is its 'centre' or 'owner'. As Berkeley puts it in the notebooks, the 'Substance of a Spirit is that it acts, causes, wills, operates, or if you please (to avoid the quibble that may be made on the word *it*), to act, cause will operate' (PC 829). Spirit *is* activity, not a thing that is active. One passage that might support this reading is PHK §143.[11] Yet another error encouraged by abstraction is that we can 'frame abstract notions of powers and acts of the mind, and consider them prescinded, as well from mind and spirit itself, and their respective objects and effects'. The second part of this statement suggests that activity cannot be conceived apart from perceived

---

[10] See Stephen H. Daniel, 'Berkeley's Christian Neoplatonism, Archetypes, and Divine Ideas', *Journal of the History of Philosophy* 39 (2001), 239–58, and Daniel, 'Berkeley's Stoic Notion of Spiritual Substance'. For a rather different version of this claim, see Robert G. Muehlmann (ed.), 'The Substance of Berkeley's Philosophy', in *Berkeley's Metaphysics: Structural, Interpretative and Critical Essays* (University Park, PA: Pennsylvania State University Press, 1995), pp. 89–105. For critical discussion of these views, see M. Hight and W. Ott, 'The New Berkeley', *Canadian Journal of Philosophy* 34 (2004), 1–24.

[11] See also PHK §98.

objects and from the creation of ideas that are the effects of activity. If we cannot conceive the two things apart from one another, then how can we grasp activity as an attribute upon which particular instances of activity depend?

Berkeley, in his notebooks, did consider a position whereby mind is just activity, rather than a thing that supports activity. A good deal of the evidence for the claim that minds are not substances but systems of activity can be adduced from this source.[12] However, this fact makes it difficult to be sure this is Berkeley's mature view, for the notebooks suggest not only this view, but attest to the fact his view was developing all the time. So, for example, among the early entries in his notebooks he considered a very radical position whereby the mind is nothing but a collection of inert ideas. We shall discuss this radical position in the next section, but the point to be made here is that even within the compass of the notebooks this position was abandoned as Berkeley began to make activity central to the self. That Berkeley was changing his view of the self in unpublished work makes it difficult to be sure what his considered position is.[13] Certainly, Berkeley seems, in the published work, to think of the mind as a 'one simple undivided, active being' (PHK 27) that is the 'substratum' of qualities (DHP3 237). Whether this is mere lip-service to the language of substance or a genuine change from the notebook view cannot be settled here. What can be safely said is that the issue of a substantial self in Berkeley and its relation to its activities remains both obscure and hotly contested.[14]

3 THE PARITY OBJECTION AND KNOWLEDGE OF SELVES

There are not only problems in trying to determine what a spirit *is* for Berkeley. There are also commitments within his system that make it obscure just how we can have knowledge of spirits, or, indeed,

---

[12] Muehlmann, 'The Substance of Berkeley's Philosophy', p. 90, suggests that the notebook view is Berkeley's real view and that talk of substance in the published work is an effort to conceal his real view to avoid offence to the Church (see pp. 104–5).

[13] This is nicely charted in Bertil Belfrage, 'Berkeley's Four Concepts of the Soul (1707–1709)', in S. Daniel (ed.), *Reexamining Berkeley's Philosophy* (University of Toronto Press, 2007), pp. 172–87.

[14] See Talia Mae Bettcher, *Berkeley's Philosophy of Spirit: Consciousness, Ontology, and the Elusive Subject* (London: Continuum, 2007), for a recent study.

whether we can really *mean* anything by the term 'spirit' and its cognates. One thing about which Berkeley is adamant is that we have no idea of spirit. He signals this early in the *Principles* (PHK §27) and returns to it at PHK §135. Malebranche had claimed the same thing, and saw it as a limitation of human understanding. Berkeley, however, does not see the idea as a defect or shortcoming (PHK §136). So why can we have no idea of spirit?

The answer is that for Berkeley ideas are necessarily inactive and spirits necessarily active, and that no passive item could possibly represent something active (PHK §§137–8). This is a consequence of the Likeness Principle, the claim that an idea can only be like an idea.[15] Since only ideas can be represented by ideas, ideas cannot represent spirits. But if we have no idea of soul, how are we able to think and talk meaningfully of souls or spirits? As Berkeley writes 'it will be objected, that if there is no idea signified by the terms *soul*, *spirit*, and *substance*, they are wholly insignificant, or have no meaning in them' (PHK §139).

This objection – and Berkeley's answer to it – is expanded upon in the *Dialogues*, where Hylas accuses Philonous of an inconsistency between his treatment of spirit and his treatment of matter, which is related to Berkeley's claim that we have no idea of spirit:

You admit . . . that there is a spiritual substance, although you have no idea of it; while you deny there can be such a thing as material substance, because you have no notion or idea of it. Is this fair dealing? To act consistently, you must either admit matter or reject spirit. (DHP3 232)

This objection is the 'Parity Objection'. Spiritual substance seems to be on a par with material substance, and if Philonous rejects the latter he must then reject the former. Philonous has a response to this objection, as we shall see, but it leaves Hylas unsatisfied, who pushes his objection further:

Notwithstanding all you have said, to me it seems, that according to your own way of thinking . . . it should follow that you are only a system of floating ideas, without any substance to support them. Words are not to be used without a meaning. And as there is no more meaning in spiritual

---

[15] See Chapter 5, section 2, pp. 71–74.

substance than in material substance, the one is to be exploded as well as the other. (DHP3 233)

It is important to understand the force of this objection. Hylas is not merely claiming not to *know* that there are spiritual substances: it is rather that we cannot attach any meaning to the words at all. So we cannot really have any argument or debate over the existence of 'spirit', since there is nothing meaningful expressed by the words. The only sense to be made of particular minds is just that of collections of 'floating ideas'. This objection would be devastating to Berkeley, and not merely because it implies that we cannot make sense of finite spirit. If we cannot make sense of finite spirit, we cannot make sense of *infinite* spirit, and, as such, we cannot make sense of God in the way Berkeley suggests we can. I have 'some sort of an active thinking image of the Deity' (DHP3 232) derived from myself. But without any conception of an active self, Berkeley cannot even begin to formulate an argument for the existence of God.

Hylas' characterisation of the self as only a 'system of floating ideas' resembles the view from the early entries in the notebooks mentioned in the previous section. Berkeley writes that 'Mind is a congeries of Perceptions. Take away Perceptions & you take away the Mind put the Perceptions and you put the mind' (PC 580).[16] The mind is just a bundle of perceptions, just as a sensible object is a collection of sensible qualities. The entries surrounding this one appeal to the lack of a meaning to explain why the mind is just a bundle of perceptions. We cannot perceive the mind, but if we are to mean something by a word, that word must be tied to what we perceive (PC 579). So when we attempt to say that 'spirit' is 'that thing wch perceives' we actually say nothing meaningful at all and are 'abus'd by the words that & thing these are vague empty words † wthout a meaning' (PC 581).[17] This argument is governed by the principle that 'no word to be used without an idea' (PC 422). But as we mentioned in the previous section, Berkeley comes to reject this austere position,

---

[16] Here there is no distinction between the act of perception and the object of that act, namely, the idea. It seems likely that in this context by 'perception' Berkeley means 'idea' qua an object.

[17] † this symbol indicates a doubt regarding the reading of the preceding word in the manuscript.

because he maintains that although we lack an idea of the self, we nevertheless possess a 'notion' of it. Thus, we:

may be said to have a notion of [active beings]. I have some knowledge or notion of my mind and its acts about ideas, inasmuch as I know or understand what is meant by those words (PHK §142)

So, Berkeley evades the objection that the word 'spirit' is meaningless by asserting that we nevertheless have a 'notion' of it. This passage is not found in the first edition of the *Principles*, and indeed the first edition makes no mention of 'notion' in connection with spirits. Furthermore, the exchange between Hylas and Philonous that both raises and attempts to answer the Parity Objection was added by Berkeley only to the third edition of *Dialogues* (where again the term 'notion' appears). In earlier editions he seems to think that we do have some understanding of those terms, but he did not explain in what that understanding consists. Thus, it is plausible that Berkeley began to realise that there was something lacking in his account, and so he introduces 'notions' in the later editions. But what are these 'notions', and how do they help?

One suggestion about how a notion can give meaning comes from Melissa Frankel.[18] She suggests that the notion of spirit gains meaning by its being *explanatory* of what we observe. To see what she is driving at let us take a look at how Philonous replies to the Parity Objection. His first response is as follows: material substance is rejected, not because we lack an idea of it, but rather because what it is supposed to be involves incoherence, that is, the unperceiving support of qualities whose existence is perception-dependent.[19] The notion of spirit, however, does not involve any incoherence. Yet this point does not tell us how the notion of spirit gets its content. Here Frankel's suggestion comes into play: Philonous states that while material substance 'can be inferred by no argument' there is nevertheless 'probability' for spirit (DHP3 233). This 'probability' is explicated by the fact that the supposition of a spirit can *explain* various phenomena. So, the suggestion goes, terms associated with notions are meaningful because we have an explanatory-based

---

[18] Melissa Frankel, 'Something-We-Know-Not-What, Something-We-Know-Not-Why: Berkeley, Meanings and Minds', *Philosophia* 37 (2009), 381–402.
[19] Cf. Chapter 5, section 4, pp. 77–79.

reason to believe that the thing referred to exists.[20] So, after Hylas suggests that the self should be considered only as a system of floating ideas, Philonous appeals to a number of things that the self might be supposed to explain. One of these is that conscious experience of objects composed of different sensible qualities also appears to have a unity, thus 'I, one and the same self, perceive both colours and sounds' (DHP3 234). Secondly, no idea itself can perceive, so there must be something else that perceives. This would tie meaning to explanation, which would chime well with the fact that Philonous says that he can 'know it by reflexion' (DHP3 233). If we introspect, we can perceive various thoughts and ideas, and can further know that there is a spirit uniting these thoughts and ideas by inference.

In support of this reading, it can be noted that Berkeley considered an explanatory justification for *material* substance. Its supposition makes it 'easier to conceive and explain the manner of' the production of ideas (PHK §19). Now Berkeley, of course, does not accept that matter explains the production of idea, but nevertheless this passage shows him considering the possibility of positing something of which we have no idea, simply on the grounds that it explains something else. An active substance, by contrast, is explanatory of a host of phenomena, including not only what we have mentioned above, but also the production of ideas. So, the suggestion goes, terms associated with notions are meaningful because we have an explana-tory-based reason to believe that the thing referred to exists.[21]

I do not, however, think this suggestion works as it currently stands. A first worry might be put in the form of a question: how can the supposition of spirit itself do any explanatory work unless we already have some understanding of spirit in the first place? The suggestion, at least as I understand it, is that 'spirit' is meaningful because its supposition is explanatory. But is it really explanatory? Supposing that there is *something that* explains, say, that the produc-tion of ideas is not the same thing as *actually explaining* their production. Saying that there must be something that explains, say, why the television is not working is not the same as actually explain-ing why it is not working. Secondly, Philonous suggests that we infer

[20] Frankel, 'Something-We-Know-Not-What', p. 401.
[21] Frankel, 'Something-We-Know-Not-What', p. 401.

a spiritual substance *from* notions, rather than treating notions themselves as implicit explanations. I cannot 'mediately from my sensations, ideas, *notions*, actions or passions, infer [matter] . . . either by probable deduction or necessary consequences. Whereas the being of myself . . . I evidently know by reflexion' (DHP3 233). So the meaning of 'notion', at least in this case, cannot be understood in terms of its capacity to explain something else, since notions are among the things to be explained. This brings us to a third point, that the passages suggest that what is inferred is a single spiritual substance, but there is something more fundamental than ideas of which we must have a notion, namely, activity *per se*. This is suggested by the passage above, where something else is inferred from a notion. We have some 'notion of . . . the operations of the mind such as willing, loving, hating' (PHK §27), a notion of an 'action' and its 'acts' in contradistinction to the mind (PHK §142). There is no suggestion here that the basic notion of activity is arrived at through an explanatory inference. So, while Frankel might be right in claiming that we arrive at the notion of a substantial self by inference, we are, nevertheless, left with the task of trying to understand the more fundamental notion of activity.

So far we have been working on the assumption that Berkeley introduced 'notions' in order to explain how terms like 'spirit' acquire a meaning, but it is in fact far from clear that this is really what he is trying to do. He seems to claim that he has some notion *because* he knows or understands words like 'spirit', telling us, 'I have some knowledge or notion of my mind, and its acts about ideas, inasmuch as I know or understand what is meant by those words' (PHK §142). The term 'notion' seems to do little but reiterate Berkeley's claim to know what 'spirit' means. Perhaps he claims this because he holds that we have direct awareness of particular instances of activity. Right at the beginning of the main part of the *Principles* Berkeley writes that it is evident that the objects of human knowledge are 'either ideas, actually imprinted on the sense, or else such as are perceived by attending to the passions or operations of the mind' (PHK §1), and we might, admittedly somewhat awkwardly, take the 'operations of the human mind' as objects of knowledge distinct from ideas.[22] Notice that this is not to say that we

---

[22] See M. R. Ayers (ed.), *George Berkeley: Philosophical Works* (Dent: London, 1975), p.77 n.1.

experience activity in *isolation* from particular ideas or bodily effects, that is, we cannot abstract the 'powers and acts of the mind ... [from] their respective objects and effects' (PHK §143). But *activity* – rather than a unitary active self – might simply be given to us in experience, and this would then result in a question about whether this activity is the activity of a single substance, requiring the kind of inference we have just discussed. However, this does not yet tell us how we can *represent* activity in thinking, even if we granted that we are directly aware of it in experience. It does not, that is, explain how we can remember or imagine our own activity. In the end, I think it becomes evident that Berkeley has no convincing response to the Parity Objection.

If knowledge of our own minds is problematic, then knowledge of other minds must be too. We 'cannot know the existence of other minds, otherwise than by their operations, or the ideas by them excited in us. I perceive several motions, changes, and combinations of ideas, that inform me there are certain particular agents like myself' (PHK §145). But if we are unsuccessful in deriving a conception of ourselves in the first place, then we cannot, in turn, conceive of agents like ourselves, let alone think that certain motions, etc. are evidence for other selves. Yet Berkeley claims we need to base our conception of other minds on our own, thus, at PHK §140, he writes that we 'know other spirits by means of our own soul, which in that sense is the image or idea of them'. Here he is using the term 'idea' in a wide sense to include 'notions', and, as we have seen, this worry goes to the heart of Berkeley's system – as we have already seen, God is another spirit whose existence is supposedly established by argument. We supposedly know that we are spirits whose activity is revealed through our command over a limited range of ideas, and, in turn, we infer that other ideas are under the command of the infinite spirit, but without any conception of self in the first place it is difficult to know how this argument can get off the ground.

There are further issues that emerge from the account of other minds offered by Berkeley. The inference to the existence of other minds is supported by the fact that the best explanation of the fact that some ideas are not under our own control is that there is some other spirit responsible for their production. Berkeley holds that this implies that 'God is known as certainly and immediately as any other mind or spirit whatsoever, distinct from ourselves.' Indeed, we 'may even assert, that the existence of God is far more evidently perceived than the existence of men; because the effects of Nature are infinitely more numerous and considerable, than those ascribed to human agents' (PHK §147), for 'the far greater part of the ideas or sensations perceived by us' are best explained by God and not by the activity of other finite spirits. But this overwhelming evidence for God threatens to swamp the supposed evidence we have for other finite spirits as causes of ideas.

We shall not pursue this problem here.[23] Let us instead note that the problem of the evidence for God's existence swamping any evidence we might have for other finite minds is compounded by the fact when finite spirits act God is involved in the production of that action. Indeed, at one point, Berkeley claims that *all* that I perceive is the consequence of His will, so that I can never perceive anything that is the direct result of the activity of some other finite spirit. Thus, he writes, it is:

evident that in affecting other persons, the will of man hath no other object, than barely the motion of the limbs of his body; but that such a motion should be attended by, or excite any idea in the mind of another, depends wholly on the will of the Creator. He alone it is who *upholding all things by the Word of his Power*, maintains that intercourse between spirits, whereby they are able to perceive the existence of each other. (PHK §147)

The effects I perceive when I supposedly see you wave your hand are, it seems, not really effects of another finite spirit at all. This, as we have seen, threatens to undermine any evidence we have for the existence of other finite spirits. But it also raises a further problem: in what sense can I be said to act in the world at all? The next section discusses why this is a problem for Berkeley, and what a solution to the problem might look like.

4 ACTION AND REALITY

For Berkeley, a spirit is an active being, whose activity centrally involves willing, while a particular act of willing is a volition.[24]

---

[23] For a good discussion of how Berkeley might actually avoid the problem, see Lorne Falkenstein, 'Berkeley's Argument for Other Minds', *History of Philosophy Quarterly* 7 (1990), 431–40.

[24] There are notorious problems with the notion of 'volition'. For discussion of the philosophical problems with it set in the context of Berkeley's philosophy, see Stoneham, *Berkeley's World*, pp. 178–81.

Particular acts of will are instances of the creation, destruction and change in ideas. Recall now that the distinction between ideas of the imagination and the ideas that constitute reality is that the former depend on my will and the latter on God's will.[25] But if only ideas of the imagination are under the command of my will, it seems that I cannot affect the world, and everything I do must be merely imaginary. Indeed, Berkeley's claim in the passage above that finite spirits have 'barely the motion of the limbs', seems too strong. Our own bodies are collections of ideas, and so if we move our bodies we do so by willing those ideas, but if they are under our control they must only be imaginary.

One way to avoid this problem is as follows: the difference between mere imagination and action is that in the latter case God causes relevant ideas in other finite spirits when I bring new ideas into creation. So when I only imagine moving my leg I simply bring certain ideas into existence in my own mind, but I 'really' move my leg when God brings about ideas in the minds of others. Action differs from imagination in that the former is public, a publicity afforded by God's activity. Such a reading is supported by phrases such as all 'depends wholly on the will of the Creator', and he 'alone . . . uphold[s] all things by the Word of His Power' and sees Berkeley embracing a position that is almost, but not quite, occasionalism. In this view, all genuine power resides with God and natural events are occasions whereby the active nature of his will is manifest. Taken to its inevitable conclusion, no finite spirits are active and so no finite spirits have the ability to act. But Berkeley must differ from this position in at least one respect, namely, that we have command over the imagination, and that is why it is almost, yet not quite, occasionalism. Nevertheless, Berkeley is ceding all other activity to God, so my imagining becomes an action in virtue of its being the *occasion* for God's active will to produce ideas in the minds of others.

If this is Berkeley's position, it carries with it a number of considerable problems. First, how are we to understand a situation where we perceive our *own* bodies moving? Take the case of moving my hand rather than merely imagining moving my hand. For it to be a case of my *moving* my hand the relevant ideas would have to be under

---

[25] Cf. Chapter 6, section 5, pp. 101–104.

my control, but in order to count as real the ideas would have to be produced by God, and therefore *not* under my control. Secondly, in objecting to a materialist form of occasionalism, Philonous asks whether 'it doth not derogate from [the wisdom and power of God] to suppose He is influenced, directed, or put in mind, when and what He is to act, by any unthinking substance' (DHP2 220), that is, to ask, how God could be affected by something from without? The same general point carries over to the position whereby our acts of will are occasions for God's activity, for it looks like acts of will must causally affect him, a thesis incompatible with the claim that God cannot be affected from without.

This worry might be softened by treating acts of will not as affecting God causally, but as covert requests or petitionary prayers. That way we are not *making* God do anything, it is rather that he is cooperating with our requests. However, this solution compounds a third problem, which is that if God alone is causally active in all action, does this not make him responsible for those actions? Hylas tells Philonous that 'in making God the immediate author of all the motions in Nature, you make him the author of murder, sacrilege, adultery, and the like heinous sins' (DHP3 236). It is God who does these wicked acts, and not us, and the fact that he does so in answer to our requests just seems to make things worse. As C. C. W. Taylor puts it, on this theory 'God does the wicked things which we want to do but are unable to do.'[26] One response to this worry given by Philonous is as follows: he argues that guilt attaches not to the 'outward physical action' but to the will. For example, since it was I that willed or intended to steal your wallet, guilt attaches to me even though the relevant sequence of ideas is the result of God's activity, and one might worry that this still makes God an accomplice in sin. To evade this worry one might hold that God's intention in realising this sequence presumably falls under the general intention of realising the will of human beings in general, rather than being the particular intention of stealing the wallet.

Philonous has a second response to this problem, and it is interesting not merely on its own terms, but because it seems to offer a

---

[26] C. C. W. Taylor, 'Action and Inaction in Berkeley', in J. Foster and H. Robinson (eds.), *Essays on Berkeley: A Tercentennial Celebration* (Oxford: Clarendon Press, 1985), p. 224.

position on action that differs from the occasionalist position with which we have so far been working. Let us examine it in full:

Lastly, I have nowhere said that God is the only agent who produces all motions in bodies. It is true, I have denied there are any other agents beside spirits: but this is very consistent with allowing to thinking rational beings, in the production of motions, the use of limited powers, ultimately indeed derived from God, but immediately under the direction of their own wills, which is sufficient to entitle them to all the guilt of their actions. (DHP3 237)

This passage explicitly denies that only God produces motion in our bodies.[27] Thus, as the last part of the quotation suggests, the guilt attaches to us rather than God because it is us that puts our bodies in motion, not him. But does this not simply return us to the same problem that the occasionalist reading tried to solve? How can I really move my body rather than merely imagine moving my body, if what constitutes the ideas of the imagination is being under the direct control of my will?

The key move in answering this question is to reject the hard dichotomy between what is caused by me and what is caused by God. Instead, Berkeley proposes a spectrum of cases. At one end is the pure imagination, the ideas that depend entirely on me, while at the other end of the spectrum are the ideas that constitute reality that I cannot at all affect by my will. Between these two extremes is a spectrum of ideas that comprise our acts and *partially* determined by my volitional activity and *partially* caused by God. In such cases, God *concurs* in the production of such actions, which contributes to their status as real events, but at the same time I am contributing causally to the production of the ideas that constitute my arm – hence, the name 'concurrentism'.[28] Philonous tells us that the 'ideas formed by the imagination' have 'an *entire* dependence on the will', whereas real things 'being imprinted on the mind by a spirit distinct from us, have not a *like* dependence on our will' (DHP3 235). Ideas of the imagination have an *entire* dependence on the will, but actions, which do depend on my will are nevertheless not *entirely* dependent on my

---

[27] 'We move our Legs ourselves, 'tis we that will their movement. Herein I differ from Malebranch' (PC 548).

[28] For this reading, see Jeffery McDonough, 'Berkeley, Human Agency and Divine Concurrence', *Journal of the History of Philosophy* 46 (2008), 567–90.

will – God is required to concur in order for me to move my body. Conversely, actions that are also real things, while not having 'a like dependence on our will', might consistently *have* a dependence on our will even though again God is required to concur in their production.

To bring out the difference between this position and the occasionalist one, consider two ways in which someone else might help me move a large piece of furniture that I cannot move myself. I could simply ask someone else to move it for me. This is like the occasionalist position. Alternatively, I could genuinely push the piece of furniture, but, because I cannot move it by myself, someone else has to push at the same time. This is like the concurrentist position. So the difference between moving my imagining and really moving my arm consists in the fact that in the latter case God cooperates in the production of such ideas, and this causal cooperation means that the ideas are real things, rather than ideas of the imagination. This position does not require there to be any other finite agent perceiving the relevant sequence of ideas in order for that sequence to account for the movement of my body, rather than my merely imagining it. It thereby avoids the problem in marking the difference between imagining and perceiving the raising of my own arm – I am active in moving my arm, but also passive to the extent to which God concurs in the sequence of ideas.

In light of this, it is possible to see Berkeley's claim in PHK §147 that human wills 'have limbs of his body' as their object at face value. We do causally affect real things (that is, our limbs), but our control of them requires the concurrence of God. We might also see Berkeley's claim that our perceiving the motions of another body depends 'wholly on the will of the Creator' as an overstatement, and instead see that God concurs in the production of such ideas while we are still able to be sensitive to other active spirits. Indeed, there are indications of a concurrentist position in the *Principles*. Thus, at PHK §145, Berkeley writes that we can know other finite minds because one can 'perceive several motions ... that inform me there are certain agents like my self, which accompany them, *and concur in their production*' (added emphasis). Perhaps this was the position that Berkeley finally settled on, but like so much in his treatment of spirits, we have no explicit treatment of it.

Bibliography

Atherton, M. *Berkeley's Revolution in Vision*. Ithaca, NY: Cornell University Press, 1990.

Atherton, M. 'The Objects of Immediate Perception', in S. Daniel (ed.), *New Interpretations of Berkeley's Thought*, Amherst, NY: Humanity Books, 2008, pp. 107–19.

Austin, J. L. *How to Do Things with Words,* 2nd edn, ed. J. O. Urmson and Marina Sbisà. Cambridge, MA: Harvard University Press, 1975.

Ayers, M. 'Was Berkeley an Empiricist or a Rationalist?', in K. Winkler (ed.), *The Cambridge Companion to Berkeley*. Cambridge University Press, 2005, pp. 34–62.

Ayers, M. R. *Locke,* 2 vols. London: Routledge, 1991.

Ayers, M. R. (ed.). *George Berkeley: Philosophical Works*. Dent: London, 1975.

Bayle, P. *Historical and Critical Dictionary, Selections*, trans. R. Popkin. Indianapolis, IN: Hackett, 1991.

Belfrage, B. 'Berkeley's Four Concepts of the Soul (1707–1709)', in S. Daniel (ed.), *Reexamining Berkeley's Philosophy*. University of Toronto Press, 2007, pp. 172–87.

Bennett, J. *Learning from Six Philosophers: Descartes, Spinoza, Leibniz, Locke, Berkeley, Hume,* 2 vols., Oxford University Press, 2001.

Bennett, J. *Locke, Berkeley, Hume: Central Themes*. Oxford University Press, 1971.

Berkeley, G. 'Editors Introduction', *A Treatise Concerning the Principles of Human Knowledge*, ed. J. Dancy, Oxford University Press, 1998.

Berman, D. *George Berkeley: Idealism and the Man*. Oxford University Press, 2002.

Bettcher, T. M. *Berkeley's Philosophy of Spirit: Consciousness, Ontology, and the Elusive Subject*. London: Continuum, 2007.

Buckle, S. 'British Sceptical Realism: A Fresh Look at the British Tradition', *European Journal of Philosophy* 7 (1999), 1–29.

Campbell, J. 'Berkeley's Puzzle', in T. Gendler and J. Hawthorne (eds.), *Conceivability and Possibility*. Oxford University Press, 2002, pp. 127–43.

Cottingham, J., Stoothoff, R. and Murdoch, D. *The Philosophical Writings of Descartes*, 2 vols., Cambridge University Press, 1985.

Cummins, P. 'Perceiving and Berkeley's Theory of Substance', in S. Daniel (ed.), *Reexamining Berkeley's Philosophy*. University of Toronto Press, 2007, pp. 121–52.

Dancy, J. *Berkeley: An Introduction*. Oxford: Blackwell, 1987.

Daniel, S. 'How Berkeley's Works are Interpreted', in S. Parigi (ed.), *George Berkeley: Religion and Science in the Age of Enlightenment*. Dordrecht: Springer, 2010, pp. 3–14.

Daniel, S. (ed.). 'Berkeley's Stoic Notion of Spiritual Substance', in *New Interpretations of Berkeley's Thought*. Amherst, NY: Humanity Books, 2008, pp. 203–30.

Daniel, S. 'Berkeley's Christian Neoplatonism, Archetypes, and Divine Ideas', *Journal of the History of Philosophy* 39 (2001), 239–58.

Dicker, G. *Berkeley's Idealism: A Critical Examination*. Oxford University Press, 2011.

Downing, L. 'Berkeley's Natural Philosophy and Philosophy of Science', in K. Winkler (ed.), *The Cambridge Companion to Berkeley*. Cambridge University Press, 2005, pp. 230–65.

Falkenstein, L. 'Berkeley's Argument for Other Minds', *History of Philosophy Quarterly* 7 (1990), 431–40.

Fogelin, R. *Berkeley and the* Principles of Human Knowledge. London: Routledge, 2001.

Frankel, M. 'Berkeley and God in the Quad', *Philosophy Compass* 7 (2012), 338–96.

Frankel, M. 'Something-We-Know-Not-What, Something-We-Know-Not-Why: Berkeley, Meanings and Minds, *Philosophia* 37 (2009), 381–402.

Gallois, A. 'Berkeley's Master Argument', *Philosophical Review* 83 (1974), 55–69.

Glauser, R. 'Berkeley on the Numerical Identity of what Several Immediately Perceive (Three Dialogues between Hylas and Philonous III 247–8), *Philosophy Compass* 7/8 (2012), 517–30.

Glauser, R. 'The Problem of the Unity of a Physical Object in Berkeley', in S. Daniel (ed.), *Reexamining Berkeley's Philosophy*. University of Toronto Press, 2007, pp. 50–81.

Grayling, A. C. *Berkeley: The Central Arguments*. La Salle, IL: Open Court, 1986.

Grice, H. P. 'Meaning', *Philosophical Review* 66 (1957), 377–88.

Hight, Marc A. *Ideas and Ontology: An Essay in Early Modern Metaphysics of Ideas.* University Park, PA: Pennsylvania State University Press, 2008.

Hight, M. and Ott, W. 'The New Berkeley', *Canadian Journal of Philosophy* 34 (2004), 1–24.

Hume, D. *A Treatise of Human Nature*, ed. L. A. Selby-Bigge, rev. P. H. Nidditch, Clarendon Press, 1978.

Jesseph, D. 'Berkeley's Philosophy of Mathematics', in K. Winkler (ed.), *The Cambridge Companion to Berkeley.* Cambridge University Press, 2005, pp. 266–310.

Jesseph, D. *Berkeley's Philosophy of Mathematics.* University of Chicago Press, 1993.

Jones, N. *Starting with Berkeley.* London: Continuum, 2009.

Kail, P. 'Causation, Fictionalism and Non-Cognitivism', in S. Parigi (ed.), *George Berkeley: Religion and Science in the Age of Enlightenment.* Dordrecht: Springer, 2010, pp. 31–40.

Kail, P. *Projection and Realism in Hume's Philosophy.* Oxford: Clarendon Press, 2007.

Kalderon, M. (ed.). *Fictionalism in Metaphysics.* Oxford: Clarendon Press, 2005.

Locke, J. *An Essay Concerning Human Understanding*, ed. P. H. Nidditch, Clarendon Press, 1975.

Loeb, L. *From Descartes to Hume: Continental Metaphysics and the Development of Modern Philosophy.* Ithaca, NY: Cornell University Press, 1981.

Lowe, E. J. 'Experience and its Objects', in T. Crane (ed.), *The Contents of Experience: Essays on Perception.* Cambridge University Press, 1992, pp. 79–104.

Luce, A. A. and Jessop, T. E. (eds.), *The Works of George Berkeley, Bishop of Cloyne,* 9 vols., London: Thomas Nelson, 1949.

McCracken, C. 'Berkeley's Notion of Spirit', in M. Atherton (ed.), *The Empiricists: Critical Essays on Locke, Berkeley and Hume.* Lanham, MD: Rowman & Littlefield, 1999, pp. 145–52.

McCracken, C. and Tipton, I. (eds.), *Berkeley's Principles and Dialogues: Background Source Materials.* Cambridge University Press, 2000.

McKim, R. 'Berkeley's Notebooks', in K. Winkler (ed.), *The Cambridge Companion to Berkeley.* Cambridge University Press, 2005, pp. 63–93.

McDonough, J. 'Berkeley, Human Agency and Divine Concurrence', *Journal of the History of Philosophy* 46 (2008), 567–90.

Malebranche, N. *Dialogues Concerning Metaphysics and Religion*, trans. N. Jolley and D. Scott. Cambridge University Press, 2007.

Malebranche, N. *The Search After Truth*, trans. T. Lennon and P. Olscamp. Cambridge University Press, 1997.

Migely, G. 'Berkeley's Actively Passive Mind', in S. Daniel (ed.), *Reexamining Berkeley's Philosophy*. University of Toronto Press, 2007, pp. 153–71.

Muehlmann, R. (ed.). 'The Substance of Berkeley's Philosophy', in *Berkeley's Metaphysics: Structural, Interpretative and Critical Essays*. University Park, PA: Pennsylvania State University Press, 1995, pp. 89–105.

Newton-Smith, W. H. 'Berkeley's Philosophy of Science', in J. Foster and H. Robinson (eds.), *Essays on Berkeley: A Tercentennial Celebration*. Oxford: Clarendon Press, 1985, pp. 149–61.

Pappas, G. *Berkeley's Thought*. Ithaca, NY: Cornell University Press, 2000.

Pitcher, G. *Berkeley*. London: Routledge, 1977.

Richmond, A. *Berkeley's Principles of Human Knowledge: A Reader's Guide*. London: Continuum, 2009.

Roberts, J. R. *A Metaphysics for the Mob: The Philosophy of George Berkeley*. New York: Oxford University Press, 2007.

Schmaltz, T. 'Malebranche's Cartesianism and Lockean Colours', *History of Philosophy Quarterly* 12 (1995), 387–403.

Schwartz, C. 'Berkeley and his Contemporaries: The Question of Mathematical Formalism', in S. Parigi (ed.), *George Berkeley: Religion and Science in the Age of Enlightenment*. Dordrecht: Springer, 2010, pp. 43–56.

Sellars, W. 'Philosophy and the Scientific Image of Man', in R. Colodny (ed.), *Science, Perception and Reality*. Ridgeview: Humanities Press, 1963.

Smith, A. D. 'Of Primary and Secondary Qualities', *Philosophical Review* 99 (1990), 221–54.

Stanley, J. 'Hermeneutic Fictionalism', in P. French and H. Wettstein (eds.), *Midwest Studies in Philosophy* xxv: *Figurative Language*. Oxford: Blackwell, 2001, pp. 36–71.

Stoneham, T. *Berkeley's World: An Examination of the Three Dialogues*. Oxford University Press, 2002.

Taylor, C. C. W. 'Action and Inaction in Berkeley', in J. Foster and H. Robinson (eds.), *Essays on Berkeley: A Tercentennial Celebration*. Oxford: Clarendon Press, 1985, pp. 211–25.

Turbayne, C. (ed.). 'Lending a Hand to Philonous: The Berkeley, Plato, Aristotle Connection', in *Berkeley: Critical and Interpretative Essays*. Manchester University Press, 1982, pp. 295–310.

Westfall, R. *The Construction of Modern Science: Mechanisms and Mechanics*. Cambridge University Press, 1971.

Williams, M. *Unnatural Doubts: Epistemological Realism and the Basis of Scepticism*. Princeton University Press, 1995.

Wilson, M. 'Did Berkeley Completely Misunderstand the Basis of the Primary–Secondary Quality Distinction in Locke?', in *Ideas and*

Mechanism: Essays on Early Modern Philosophy. Princeton University Press, 1999, pp. 215–28.

Winkler, K. *Berkeley: An Interpretation*. Oxford: Clarendon Press, 1989.

Woolhouse, R. *Descartes, Spinoza, Leibniz: The Concept of Substance in Seventeenth-Century Metaphysics*. London: Routledge, 1993.

Yolton, J. *John Locke and the Way of Ideas*. Oxford: Clarendon Press, 1956.

Index

For EU product safety concerns, contact us at Calle de José Abascal, 56–1°, 28003 Madrid, Spain or eugpsr@cambridge.org.